BOOKKEEPERS' BOOT CAMP:
Get a Grip on Accounting Basics

Angie Mohr, CA, CMA

BOOKKEEPERS' BOOT CAMP: Get a Grip on Accounting Basics

Angie Mohr, CA, CMA

Self-Counsel Press
(a division of)
International Self-Counsel Press Ltd.
USA Canada

Self-Counsel Press acknowledges the financial support of the Government of Canada through the Canada Book Fund (CBF) for our publishing activities.

First edition: 2003; Reprinted: 2004 (2); 2006; 2007

Second edition: 2010

Library and Archives Canada Cataloguing in Publication

Mohr, Angie
Bookkeepers' boot camp: get a grip on accounting basics / Angie Mohr. — 2nd ed.

ISBN 978-1-77040-044-3

1. Bookkeeping. 2. Small business--Accounting. I. Title.
HF5636.M63 2010 657'.9042 C2010-900023-4

Printed in Canada

Self-Counsel Press
(a division of)
International Self-Counsel Press Ltd.

1704 North State Street
Bellingham, WA 98225
USA

1481 Charlotte Road
North Vancouver, BC V7J 1H1
Canada

Contents

Figure

Samples

Worksheets

Notice to Readers

Laws are constantly changing. Every effort is made to keep this publication as current as possible. However, the author, the publisher, and the vendor of this book make no representations or warranties regarding the outcome or the use to which the information in this book is put and are not assuming any liability for any claims, losses, or damages arising out of the use of this book. The reader should not rely on the author or the publisher of this book for any professional advice. Please be sure that you have the most recent edition.

Acknowledgments

So many ingredients are essential to the creation of a book. Without the convergence of a great publisher, editor, family, and friends, this book would most certainly still be a pile of papers stacked in my living room.

Thanks go to Richard, Judy, and everyone at Self-Counsel Press who supported this project from the beginning and saw it all the way through.

Many thanks to all of my clients, both in my accounting practice and of our online products and services. You have taught me so much over the years. I hope that this book lives up to your expectations. I wrote it for you.

For their general support, encouragement, and the occasional beer, I would like to thank Dave Sturgeon, Andrew Pyper, John Weir, Hayley Chandler, Ali Sammel, Tim and April Bartlett, Lindsay Mund, and Yesenia Torres.

Most of all, I would like to thank my family, without whose support, babysitting, and hugs, this book would not have been possible. I dedicate this book to my husband, Jeff, and my two perfect angels, Alex and Erika.

THE BASICS

Chapter 1

Getting Started

The statistics are mind numbing. In North America, 80 percent of all small businesses started this year will be gone in five years. Of the lucky 20 percent to have survived, another 80 percent will be gone in ten years. That's a whopping 96 percent failure rate over ten years.

Would you start a small business if you were told that you have a 96 percent chance of failure? Not many people would. But every day, hundreds of people think they will beat the odds. They may be former employees, students, housewives, or others who have never had any business training but are sure that their product or service is so fantastic, so completely unique, that they are destined to succeed.

These are the people who walk through the doors of my accounting and consulting practice every day. They want to know how to make a lot of money, how to leverage their businesses, how to go public. I begin to talk to them about their plans for bookkeeping for the business ("Oh, my wife will sort all that out"), what is in their business plan ("Oh, I'll pull one of those together if the bank is looking for one"), and what their break-even point is ("We don't have to worry about any of that; this product is going to sell millions!"). They want to fly before they've learned to crawl. They do not understand that business management is a separate skill from doing whatever it is that their business does. For example, hairdressers think that because they are good at cutting hair, they can own and manage a salon. Lawyers think that because they are good at putting together a brief, they can run a ten-lawyer law practice.

Am I being hard on small business? Not at all. Small business is the engine of the world economy. Even Microsoft and Ford started in someone's basement or garage. However, people all over the world have

CASE STUDY

Joe gets up when the alarm goes off at 5:45 a.m. His once-tiny plumbing business has grown substantially over the last year, and Joe always feels as if he's in catch-up mode. He knows he has a lot of work to do today. A presentation will be made to a potential customer at 9:30 a.m., a meeting with his banker has been set up for 11:00 a.m., he must personally pick up a product from a supplier at 2:00 p.m., and at 3:30 p.m., he must deal with a cranky customer who is not happy with the quality of Joe's work.

Joe makes his daily rounds after stopping at Starbucks for a double hit of espresso. He telephones his wife, Becky, from his cell phone to remind her to pull the invoices to discuss with the customer that afternoon. Becky stays home and helps Joe run the business. She answers the phone, does the filing, and deals with the mountains of paperwork that the business generates.

At 6:00 p.m., when Joe has finished his rounds for the day, he pulls the truck into his driveway, slings his jacket over his shoulder, and checks in with Becky. He tells his wife that the banker wants to see financial statements for the business to see if they are making money. Neither Joe nor Becky really knows if they are winning or losing. Becky adds up all the receipts at the end of the year for the income tax returns. As she tells him about the phone calls she received during the day and the bank statement that appears to be wrong, Joe digs through his pants pockets and pulls out piles of crumpled receipts: the day's record keeping. Becky tries to put them in some semblance of order, wondering if there's a better way to track the business results.

an idealized and unrealistic view of how to operate a business, and most discount the importance of the basics. With the advent of bookkeeping software such as *Simply Accounting and QuickBooks,* many entrepreneurs have come to believe that these programs will magically do their bookkeeping for them. Because these people lack basic accounting skills, they are unable to analyze their business results and have no idea what's working and what's not. It's like driving a car in a foreign country where they can't understand what the road signs are telling them.

The *Numbers 101 for Small Business* Series

Over the years, my clients have asked me to recommend good books on small-business management and accounting. I have always found it difficult to do so, as most books on the subject are either dry textbooks or too general to be of any use.

This problem was the genesis of the *Numbers 101 for Small Business* series of books. The series functions as an easy-to-understand reference for small-business owners, and covers such topics as bookkeeping, analyzing, and tracking financial information, as well as the complexities of starting, growing, and exiting a business. The series is distilled from the workshops, radio broadcasts, and one-to-one training sessions I have conducted in my accounting firm over the years. You, the small-business owner, will find within this series everything you need to base your business on sound financial and management principles. Throughout this book, you will meet Joe and his wife, Becky. Joe owns a small business called (appropriately) Joe's Plumbing. Becky does the back-office work for the business: answering phones, invoicing, bookkeeping, and banking. You will learn how Joe worked with his accountant to strengthen his business and make it more profitable and risk proof. You will find samples of financial documents and other useful tools that you can customize to your business needs. More information and tools can be found on my website: www.numbers101.com.

Bookkeepers' Boot Camp

Bookkeepers' Boot Camp, the book you are reading now, is the first book in the *Numbers 101 for Small Business* series. It deals with the essentials of record keeping for a small business and will show you why it's necessary for you to track financial information. By the end of this book, you will have a greater understanding of the purpose and process of record keeping and a deeper understanding of your business and how it works.

I wish you the best in your business. You have taken a significant first step in understanding your business better. Drop me a line at angie@numbers101.com and let me know how your business is doing. I'd love to hear from you!

How to Use This Book

Bookkeepers' Boot Camp is broken into three sections:

1. The Basics

Chapters 2 through 7 start with the fundamentals of record keeping. This section is a great place to start for those who are just beginning to learn bookkeeping. It's also a great refresher for those who have been doing it for a while. You will learn the basic methods of record keeping for a growing business and the statements that make up the financials.

2. Intermediate Topics

Chapters 8 through 18 show you the "meat and potatoes" of bookkeeping. You will learn how to record the sales and purchases cycles, account for the everyday transactions that a business undertakes, as well as learn how to balance the bank account and what to do if you can't reconcile it.

3. Advanced Issues

Now that you are all warmed up and have a good handle on the regular financial workings of your business, it's time to sink your teeth into more advanced topics. In Chapters 19 through 23, you will learn how to deal with foreign currency, tax planning, budgeting, and the role of the external accountant. Following these chapters comes Chapter 24: Graduation, an integrated self-test you can take to see if you really know your stuff!

Throughout the book, you will find some useful samples of financial documents, as well as a listing of terminology and definitions in Appendix A. Appendix B lists some useful websites, publications, and other tools for small businesses.

Do you have to read everything in the order in which it appears? Of course not (unless you are fanatical like me and have a deep-rooted need to follow things in the order intended). You can review the Table of Contents and just jump right in wherever you feel that you will get the most benefit. I do recommend, however, that you eventually read the entire book, even if you already have some bookkeeping experience. You may find that you gain some new philosophical or mechanical perspectives on your business.

Once you are finished *Bookkeepers' Boot Camp,* you are ready for the next challenge: *Financial Management 101: Get a Grip on Your Business Numbers*. This book is the second in the *Numbers 101 for Small Business* series. *Financial Management 101* builds on your basic bookkeeping knowledge so that you can track and interpret your financial statements and manage your business more effectively.

I hope you enjoy *Bookkeepers' Boot Camp*. Please also visit my website at www.numbers101.com for more resource links and other cool tools for businesses. There is a place to sign up for our free e-newsletter, chock full of useful information for business owners. There is also a link to my email. Please feel free to drop me a line and let me know what you liked and didn't like about this book. It will help us develop future editions so that we can meet the needs of entrepreneurs better.

Now, if you're ready, grab a fresh cup of coffee, and let's begin!

Chapter 2

A Brief Look at the Origins of Bookkeeping

Perhaps you're not as excited as I am about the long and prestigious history of bookkeeping. Fair enough. But a brief look at the historical need for and development of record keeping in business will help you to understand bookkeeping's place in your business.

Although accounting as we know it has existed for only about 150 years, financial record keeping can be traced back more than 6,000 years. There has always been a need to be able to express someone's wealth to others to provide some kind of a net worth statement. Sophisticated record keeping developed only after two concepts came into common usage: the invention of coinage and the development of the Arabic numbering system.

In ancient times, most record keeping consisted of a listing of assets:

4 pieces of gold

2 goats

12 chickens

You can see how it would be difficult to compare the asset list of one person to another, when there is no common basis of worth. How many chickens does one goat get you? Four? Ten?

In the second millennium BCE, the Chinese invented coinage: pieces of metal that carried a government stamp verifying their value. Once this standard unit of account existed, it became possible to express value by using numbers and to compare relative net worth and transactional values. Look at the following example:

4 pieces of gold = 12 units of money

2 goats = 6 units of money

12 chickens = 9 units of money

Total net worth = 27 units of money

There still existed the problem of trade among peoples with different coinage. Each would have to determine the relative values of their money against the money of other peoples. We still face that issue today with foreign exchange.

The second major breakthrough in both mathematics and accounting was the development of the Arabic numbering system. This system was not widespread in Europe until the thirteenth century ACE. The Arabic system brought standard place values to numbering systems, which allowed numbers to be lined up in columns, making addition and subtraction much easier.

Once these two important concepts came into use, bookkeeping prospered. The need grew great in the thirteenth century. International trade flourished between the Middle East and Europe. The Italians were at the forefront of trade expeditions and also of banking. They developed systems to track lending and revenues. During this time, the nature of business also slowly started to change from individual transactions to long-term partnerships, and it therefore became necessary to track investment capital for the partners.

Double-Entry Bookkeeping

We will talk a lot in the upcoming chapters about double-entry bookkeeping. It is the basis for modern record keeping. The basic tenet of double-entry is that for every transaction, at least two accounting events are triggered. For example, when goods are purchased for cash, there is both a decrease in cash and an increase in the purchase account. These entries "balance" each other; in other words, they are equal and offsetting.

Double-entry bookkeeping has its natural origins in the thirteenth-century sea voyages venturing out of Europe. Wealthy merchants would partner together and commission a voyage to the East, to exchange their wares for silk, spices, and other exotic merchandise. The captain of the ship would have control and responsibility over the goods, from the time the ship left port until it returned to Europe. When the ship returned, the captain would be required by the merchants to account for the trip: to "balance" the goods unsold with the sales proceeds, which were either cash or other goods. In other words, if the ship left with a cargo valued at 10,000 lira, it would be expected to return with that value, split between unsold goods, new goods, and money.

Along came Friar Luca Pacioli in 1494. He wanted to capture the accounting practices of the time and he wrote an extensive treatise on the subject. This document was the first "how-to" book for double-entry bookkeeping and it was considered the standard for accounting practices for almost 200 years.

How does this history relate to you and your small business? Record keeping is as important as ever. You need to report your business transactions to shareholders, lenders, and taxation authorities. Accurate accounting is even more relevant in today's electronic age, when money is "transferred" in a nanosecond electronically.

The next chapter deals with what you need to track and how to set up your bookkeeping system for your small business.

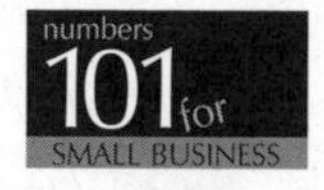

Chapter 3

Important Concepts

Before you jump into setting up and maintaining a bookkeeping system, there are several important things you must keep in mind. These are fundamental concepts that will help to guide you through your reporting and control process, and also help you to troubleshoot problems as they arise. These concepts are in no particular order nor will I give you the dry textbook backgrounds of how they came into being. Lucky you!

Generally Accepted Accounting Principles (GAAP)

Every country in the world that has an organized stock exchange has what are called Generally Accepted Accounting Principles (GAAP). These are rules or guidelines that accountants and bookkeepers are required to follow for the recording of transactions. To be listed on the stock exchange, all publicly traded companies are required to follow these rules. Smaller companies are generally required to use them for income tax purposes (though there can be some differences between accounting principles for financial statements and tax returns). You can think of GAAP as the *right* way to do things. It is also, for some companies, the *legal* way to do things.

In the United States, the independent body that governs these standards is the Financial Accounting Standards Board; in Canada, it's the Canadian Accounting Standards Board; in England, the Accounting Standards Board UK; and in Australia, the Australian Accounting Standards Board.

How do you know if you are recording your transactions in accordance with GAAP? Books like this one can be a valuable resource. You can also discuss your record keeping system with your accountant, whose job it is to keep on top of GAAP and any changes that occur within it.

Stewardship

One of your principal roles as bookkeeper (whether or not you are also the company's owner) is that of steward over the assets of the company. What this means is that your job is to account for the company's assets and any changes to those assets. You are reporting this information to four major users of the financial statements:

Owners: The company's owners want to know exactly what the company owns and how much profit it has made. It's easy to understand why they want this information. Ultimately, they are the beneficiaries of the assets and the profits. Their goal is to make sure that the assets are still there within the company, producing a lot of profit.

Investors: Many companies have external investors who invest money in the corporation in exchange for a share of the profits down the road. They have the same goals and the same need for information as the owners do.

Lenders: During the start-up period, most companies have to borrow money to operate. The lenders of this money may be banks, other companies, or individuals. The lenders' concern is whether or not the company will be able to produce enough money to pay them back. They want financial information that shows them what the company's assets are (in case the lenders need to foreclose on them), what other types of debt the company has, and how much the company is making and paying out to the owners.

Taxation Authorities: In the US, this body is the Internal Revenue Service; in Canada, it's Canada Revenue Agency; and in the UK, it's HM Revenue & Customs. No matter what it's called, the government is very interested in your company's financial information. It wants to make certain the company (or the owners, if the company is not incorporated) pays tax on all the profit and capital employed in the business. They're most interested in the recording of revenues and expenses. It's from these numbers that the taxation body derives its own income.

As you can see, the bookkeeping information that you produce will have many users, and they all have different needs and goals. It's important for you to track the accounting cycle in such a way that all users' needs are satisfied. Doing so will also help you give your company's managers information to help them make better decisions.

Accrual Accounting

This is a very important concept, as most financial information is tracked on an accrual basis. (Your accountant can discuss any exceptions to this general rule with you.)

The principle underlying accrual accounting is matching. The matching principle says that income and expenses should be recorded in the period to which they relate, not necessarily the period in which cash actually changes hands. Here are some examples of accrual accounting:

1. A customer buys product from you in January but she does not pay you until March. The conditions for the sale were met in January (i.e., she

came and picked up the product), so the sale would be recorded in January. Instead of cash, you have generated another asset: accounts receivable.

2. You start your business in September and pay your business insurance premium for the period September 1 to August 31. The insurance cost that relates to September is only one-twelfth of the premium paid, not the whole amount of the payment.
3. You pay your employees every two weeks. You have a December 31 year-end and your last paychecks go out on December 26, covering the two-week period ending December 24. There is still seven days worth of salary expense in December not yet paid for (the 25th to the 31st). You would make an adjustment to accrue that salary in the current year, not in the next year, when it will actually be paid out. Instead of a credit to the bank, you have created a liability to pay employees.

Debits and Credits

When you read a map, you talk about north, south, east, and west. When you read accounting, you talk about debits and credits. Debits and credits are the fundamental directional markers in accounting, and both terms will be used often in this book.

Before proceeding, however, one rather confusing concept must be explained. The only other place you are likely to see debits and credits is on your bank statements. In bank terminology, when money goes into your account, it's a credit; when it comes out, it's a debit. In the world of accounting, the debits and credits relating to your bank account are the opposite. When you account for an outflow from your bank account, you will credit the balance. When you have an inflow, you debit it. Once you've worked with bank statements and bookkeeping for a while, this concept won't seem so strange.

Accountants versus Bookkeepers

You undoubtedly have heard the terms "accountant" and "bookkeeper" in many different contexts in your lifetime. Many people use these terms interchangeably. However, there are some general fundamental differences between the two roles. Accountant has a much broader meaning, whereas bookkeeper is focused mainly on transactional recording. What follows is a list of some of the roles each plays in an organization.

Bookkeeper

- Controls the source documents that come into the business
- Records detailed bookkeeping entries to account for the transactions of the business
- Prepares a trial balance at the end of every period to be reviewed by management
- Records the adjusting journal entries prepared at the end of every period, such as depreciation, asset reserves, and bad debts

Accountant

May perform all the above duties, plus the following:

- Reviews detailed bookkeeping transactions and summaries to detect errors or omissions
- Presents and interprets summary financial information for senior management

- Designs the internal control processes of the company to assist in day-to-day operations and to prevent fraud
- Projects the future growth of the business
- Provides explanations for differences between the actual performance of the business and projections

If you are a one-person show in your small business, these distinctions don't matter. You are both the accountant and the bookkeeper, as well as manager, salesperson, credit department, marketing department, and chief bottle washer!

Accounting Jargon

Accounting terminology is plentiful and confusing, so throughout the book, I will try to minimize its use. However, there will be times when it will be of value for you to pick up and learn a new term. Just as when you visit a foreign country, learning a few key phrases will help your trip go smoothly and can help you communicate with the natives!

The Use of Estimates

At first glance, it will seem as if bookkeeping is a very exact science, with each number coming from a specific source document. However, there are many instances in which estimates are used in accounting. These estimates are made with as much information as possible, but still contain some subjective reasoning. Some examples are bad debt reserves, accrued liabilities, inventory obsolescence, and goodwill amortization.

When you read the financial statements of other companies, you should keep in mind that those statements have been prepared using these types of estimates. In fact, in public companies, there can be great debate among the management, the external auditors, and the investors as to which estimates should be used in the final statements!

The Importance of Bookkeeping

I am not going to waste space in this book trying to convince you that detailed transactional recording is fun, life enhancing, or personally fulfilling. There are some people who think so, and these people make a career of bookkeeping for others. That's not who you are. You are an entrepreneur running a small business, trying to muck through all the legal and taxation requirements.

However, I will take a few moments to discuss how crucial "taking care of the books" is. I have seen hundreds of small-business owners who didn't understand the importance of record keeping and always put it off until "later." "Later" rarely happens until it's too late. These business owners are almost literally buried under a pile of papers, overwhelmed by the immensity of the task at hand, being threatened by various levels of government because they are late filing returns, and too afraid to answer their phones for fear it's a creditor demanding payment for a bill that is somewhere in that pile. Not only are these people not planning and growing their businesses, they are also simply juggling paper, hoping to keep the doors open.

I implore you right from the beginning to take your bookkeeping seriously. It can be the difference between bankruptcy and success. You can't know how you're doing until you record it.

If you feel that you cannot keep up with the bookkeeping or do not have the patience to deal with it, by all means, hire a bookkeeper (there will be more about that in later chapters). Do not pile all your papers in a shoe box (or a refrigerator box!), hoping that magic little bookkeeping fairies will come along and make it all go away. It's much more likely that the Wicked Witch of the West (in the form of government auditors) will show up and "help" you with your mess. That form of help could cost you thousands of dollars in interest and late-filing penalties. Save yourself the grief and get on top of your bookkeeping today.

Setting up the Record Keeping System

In this chapter, you will learn —

- What your basic source documents are
- What kind of information you need to track
- The pros and cons of different record-keeping systems
- The pros and cons of manual versus computerized systems

Every business generates mountains of paperwork, also called source documents. Most of these provide critical backup for the entries that will be made in the accounting system. It's important right from the beginning that you set up a system to track, record, and store these documents for internal management and external taxation purposes.

Time and time again in my accounting practice, I see small businesses that are literally buried in paperwork. They know enough to hang on to the paper, but do not know how to control it. Every large company has documented systems for filing and recording source documents (i.e., bills, receipts, invoices, and bank statements), and if you want to succeed in business, you should too.

What Kinds of Paper Do I Need to Keep?

Let's break down source documents by type.

Invoices

Every time you make a sale to a customer, you will generate an invoice that describes all the information regarding the sale: the date, what was sold, the amount, any taxes, and payment terms. If you run a retail business with a cash register, your register tapes function as invoices.

You will need at least two and probably three copies of every invoice. The customer will get one for his or her records (to enter it into his or her accounting system) and you will need to keep one so that you can

CASE STUDY

Becky eyed the stack of file folders on the corner of the desk. She had set up the folders at the beginning of the year to hold all the receipts and bank statements. Now it was almost the end of the year, and Becky knew that she would have to add them all up for the tax returns.

The phone rang once more, and Becky glanced again at the folders while she set up an appointment for Joe to go fix a leak in a customer's sink. How would she ever find time to put them all in order and add them up? She wasn't even sure she had them all. Sometimes, Joe would come home from a long day of appointments and dump out his pockets on the table. Among the mints, lint, and nickels were receipts for gas, coffee, and supplies. Who knew if they were all there? Joe would take $20 out of the business bank account, but the receipts he brought back never seemed to total that much. She had to figure out how to track things better.

Becky picked up the business card she had gotten from a friend and fellow businesswoman. The card was for an accountant — one highly recommended by her friend. Becky knew the business was getting too big for her and Joe to handle without help. She called the accountant.

record it in your accounting system. You may choose to generate a third copy to keep in your accounts receivable folder until paid. This way, you will have one set of records ordered by date sale was made (most useful for accounting purposes) and one set of records ordered by date money was received (most useful for tracking cash flow).

Statements of account

You will undoubtedly have customers who owe you money at the beginning of every month. It is a good idea to send them a statement of account monthly so that they can see how much they still owe you, how old the invoice is, and the details of any payments that have been applied to their accounts. A statement of account is like a snapshot: a picture of all transactions that have occurred to date with that particular customer.

Deposit slips

When a customer pays you, you will have to deposit the money into your business bank account. To do this, you will prepare a deposit slip. Although some banks do not require you to use deposit slips, you should prepare them anyway, as they are an accurate record of who has paid you. Think of what would happen if you received checks from four customers on the same day. If the amount is just shown as a lump sum on your bank statement, how will you remember two months from now where the money came from? Prepare a deposit slip.

Supplier invoices

Every time you purchase anything for your business, you must make certain you get an invoice or a cash register receipt. If your taxation authority ever audits you, it will require you to produce the original receipt to prove that, say, the $5,000 you are claiming really was a business expense and not your personal trip to Maui. Also, your accounting system may require you to account for the taxes you pay on the expense; the supplier invoice provides that breakdown.

Check stubs or copies

When you write a business check to a supplier, you should keep a copy of that check for your records. Many check styles include a check stub: the piece that stays in your checkbook after you tear off the check. The stub has spaces to record all the information that would have appeared on the check you just wrote, including to whom the check was written, the date, the total payment, and the tax portion. If you choose to use a manual accounting system, you will use these check stubs to enter your supplier payments.

Some check systems print three copies of each check: the actual check, an attached copy for the recipient, and a third copy for the sender. In this case, you would save the third copy to keep in check order.

Purchase orders

You may or may not use purchase orders in your business. When you order goods from a supplier, you may fill out a purchase order first. This order would not include prices but would show the quantities and types of goods you ordered. You may also receive purchase orders from your customers. If so, you would keep these with your invoices, making sure that what your customer ordered was what you supplied.

Bank statements

For most business accounts, you will receive a bank statement at the end of the month showing the activity for that month. This paper will be one of your critical control documents for your business. You will need to reconcile your accounting system to your bank statements to make sure that you have accounted for every transaction.

Canceled checks

Along with your bank statement, you will most likely receive all the checks you wrote that were cashed during that month. You should keep these in case you ever have to prove to a supplier that you paid an invoice. The bank stamp on the back of the check carries information as to when and where the check was cashed.

How Do I Account for My Source Documents?

Now that you know which types of documents to keep, you need to know what to do with them.

The basic purpose of any bookkeeping system is to record the transactions of the business. In the previous chapter, you learned that all bookkeeping transactions have at least two sides; in other words, at least two things change simultaneously. You can think of it in terms of increases and decreases. When you sell your product, you increase your sales and you also increase your bank balance (if you sell for cash) or your accounts receivable balance (if you sell on credit). In bookkeeping, increases and decreases are expressed as debits (DR) and credits (CR). Depending on the type of account you are affecting, you will either be debiting or crediting that account. There are four main types of accounts in any system:

- **Assets:** Increases debit the account, and decreases credit the account
- **Liabilities:** Increases credit the account, and decreases debit the account
- **Expenses:** Increases debit the account, and decreases credit the account

- **Revenues:** Increases credit the account, and decreases debit the account

Assets and expenses are affected the same way because they both represent outflows of cash. When you spend money, you are either paying for an expense or buying an asset. Liabilities and revenues are affected the same way because they both represent inflows of cash. When money comes in, you have either sold something or you are borrowing funds.

Let's look at an example: You go to the office supply store to buy pens and paper for your office for $37.50. You pay for the purchase with the company debit card. (We will ignore taxes for now.) When you get back to your office, you will record the transaction:

DR Office supplies (an expense)	**$37.50**	
CR Bank (an asset)		**$37.50**

You are increasing your expenses and decreasing your bank account by the same amount. One of the fundamental principles in accounting is that for any given transaction, DEBITS EQUAL CREDITS. You can see this principle at work in the example above. You have increased your office supplies by the exact amount that you have decreased your bank account. It's like the principle of cause and effect. For every action, there is a reaction. (Okay, I know I'm paraphrasing heavily but you get the point!)

Let's look at another example: You sell some of your inventory to a customer for $475.25. They will not pay you for another 30 days. Notice that even though your customer has not paid you yet, the sale has still occurred and needs to be accounted for. Your entry would be as follows:

DR Accounts receivable	**$475.25**	
CR Sales		**$475.25**

You have simultaneously increased your receivables balance and your sales.

Where Do I Record This Information?

Now you know what you need to record. But where do you record it?

Whether you use a manual accounting system or a computerized accounting system, the following information applies. The only difference is that with a computerized system, much of the actual debits and credits are done in the background behind the scenes and may be transparent to you. It's important, however, that you first get a solid understanding of the mechanics of bookkeeping so that you will be able to troubleshoot any out-of-balance or other annoying problems.

Journals and ledgers

A journal is the place where you record transactions. A ledger is the place where you record summaries of changes.

There can be several journals; the sales journal (where all sale transactions are recorded), the purchases journal (where purchases are recorded), and the general journal (where everything else is recorded). Most small businesses have only a general journal and post all entries in there, so that is what is used in the following examples. The two examples above would be posted into the general journal as shown in Sample 1.

Each general journal entry is numbered GJ1, GJ2, and so forth. The posting reference (that is, the number stated below the account name) shows the balance sheet or income statement account to which an individual line will post. In Sample 1, 1-1500 is the

Sample 1

GENERAL JOURNAL

Date	Entry #	Bank DR	Bank CR	Bank (bal)	A/R DR/(CR)	Revenue CR	Office Supplies DR
		1-1000	1-1000		1-1500	4-1000	5-1250
				193.12			
17 Feb	GJ1		37.50	155.62			37.50
28 Feb	GJ2				475.25	475.25	

accounts receivable account. Remember that the debits must always equal the credits in any journal entry.

At some point — usually at the end of the month — the general journal entries are posted into the general ledger. The general ledger will have a page for each balance sheet and income statement account, and that page will show only the pieces of journal entries that affect that particular account. The general ledger will always give you a running balance of each of your accounts. Because everything you enter into the journals (and, ultimately, the ledgers) balances, when you add up all the ending balances of all your accounts, they will also balance. If they do not balance, you have made an input error in your recording. Sample 2 shows how these entries will look posted in the general ledger (assuming there were no other transactions in the month).

Also at the end of the accounting cycle, you will need to prepare a trial balance, which is simply a listing of all accounts (assets, liabilities, equity, revenue, and expenses) at the end of the period. It is called a trial balance because it is a testing of your records to make certain they balance. This trial balance will be the basis of your basic financial statements: the balance sheet and the income statement. (These will be discussed in Chapters 5 and 6.)

What Kind of Bookkeeping System Should I Get?

There are many choices when it comes to business bookkeeping systems. You can use a manual system in which you write the details of the transactions in journals and manually post them into ledgers. You can also purchase one of the myriad of computer software programs that perform accounting for small businesses. It can be difficult to decide what's best for you. Let's look at the pros and cons of some of these systems.

Manual journal and ledger

This is usually the least expensive solution but the most time consuming. You will need to purchase at least two books: a general

Sample 2

GENERAL LEDGER

1-1000	Bank			
Date	Description	DR	CR	Balance
				193.12
28 Feb	Month end		37.50	155.62

1-1500	Accounts Receivable			
Date	Description	DR	CR	Balance
				0.00
28 Feb	Month end	475.25		475.25

4-1000	Revenue			
Date	Description	DR	CR	Balance
				0.00
28 Feb	Month end		475.25	475.25

5-1250	Office Supplies			
Date	Description	DR	CR	Balance
				0.00
28 Feb	Month end	37.50		37.50

journal and a general ledger. You can purchase these from most office supply stores.

The general journal will be a large wire-bound book with 8, 16, or 32 columns. In it, you will record the details of your transactions. Each column will represent either a balance sheet or income statement item.

The general ledger is usually a three-ring binder containing ledger sheets. Each sheet represents a balance sheet or income statement item. The monthly summaries from the general journal are posted in the general ledger, which keeps a running total of each account balance.

Take a look at Sample 1 for an example of a typical general journal page. Note that most accounts have only either a debit or a credit column, depending on the nature of the item. For example, revenue is a credit; all expenses are debits. Any unusual transaction, such as returned goods or a refund of insurance premiums, that required a debit to revenues or a credit to an expense would be shown with brackets around it.

Exceptions to this rule are the bank columns. Here you have both a debit and a credit column as well as a balance column, because there can be either debits or credits to the bank with regular frequency. The balance column allows you to keep track of your cash at any moment.

Note also that in this system, each row nets out to zero, meaning that the debits equal the credits, following the basic accounting principles described in Chapter 3.

At the end of the month, you will total all of the columns and post the totals to the general ledger.

The benefit of this type of ledger and journal system is its low cost; however, you may find that the time that you spent bookkeeping could have been spent more profitably on income-generating activities for your company. Not only will it take you longer to post the transactions after they have occurred, you must also handwrite (or type on a typewriter) all of your invoices, customer statements, checks, and letters to customers and suppliers.

Computerized bookkeeping systems

If you go into any office supply store, you will find many accounting packages for small businesses. Three of the largest international players in the small-business software arena are *MYOB (Mind Your Own Business)*, *QuickBooks*, and *Simply Accounting*. There are dozens of others, each with benefits and drawbacks, but these three are the big ones. How do you know which will be the best for your business?

There are a few things you can do to minimize the risk of choosing a program that doesn't meet your needs:

- Read the back of the software box to learn about the main features of each program.
- Talk to other business owners in your industry. Some software works better for certain industries than for others.
- Talk to your accountant. Accountants are often familiar with the benefits and downfalls of many of the popular programs. However, make sure that your accountant is familiar with multiple systems; people sometimes simply recommend the only system with which they are familiar.
- Try demonstration versions. Go onto each software developer's website. Many developers have demo versions that you can try, or at least have screen shots of the program's main features. This information will give you a feel for what the program does, before you invest in it.
- Make sure that you understand whether or not the program will require you to upgrade every year. Some of the popular programs require that you keep current with the new payroll tables (which they sell you every six months to a year) or other features. Other programs will allow you to override outdated functionality. Be certain that you know how much upgrades will cost you so that you have no surprises later.

- Make sure that the company that produces the software is large enough and stable enough to be around five years from now. You do not want to discover that you have tracked all your business transactions in a program that no longer exists and which cannot be exported to another program. Manual conversion can be costly.

The main drawback of computerized systems is the cost. Not only do you have to purchase the software program (and perhaps upgrade frequently), but you also need to make sure that you have an adequate computer system and a printer to print out your reports.

The benefits of computerized systems are many:

- Much of the actual debiting and crediting happens behind the scenes in the program. For example, when you record an invoice, it looks like an invoice on the screen.
- Your balance sheet and income statement appear at the touch of a button. They are automatically generated from the transactional detail.
- Your invoices, customer statements, checks, and letters to customers and suppliers are generated from the accounting system. There are two benefits: they look more professional coming from the computer, and you save yourself a step. For example, when you prepare an invoice in your accounting system, you print off a copy for your customer, and the software automatically records it in the accounts receivable system. In a manual system, you would have to handwrite the invoice and post it to the books after the fact.
- Searching for historical transactions is easy. Most programs have a "find transaction" function that allows you to go directly to entries that you have made in the past. No flipping pages.
- Most programs have warning functions. For example, if you are recording a credit sale to a customer that is in excess of their credit limit, the system will warn you as you are writing up the sale. It is much easier to track credit terms, outstanding receivables, and other critical customer information with a computerized system.
- Most of the systems will walk you through the initial setup process with "wizards." The system asks you a number of questions regarding your business and automatically sets up the recording system based on your industry and your preferences.

As you can see, there are many considerations to take into account in the initial setup process for your bookkeeping system. However, it is comforting to know that you have so many options. Another comforting fact is that no choice is permanent. If you start with a manual system and, after six months, find it too onerous, you can convert your bookkeeping over to a computerized system relatively easily. If you despise the software that you purchased, most accounting software has a conversion function that will import your accounting history and customer and vendor lists with a few clicks of the mouse.

Take some time to consider your method up front, but know that you can always change it later on.

CASE STUDY

Becky brought Vivian, the new accountant, another coffee. Becky couldn't wait for Joe to come home. Vivian had been there for two hours. The first hour, she asked Becky many questions about their business and how they were operating it. Becky showed Vivian the stacks of file folders and the accounts receivable list taped to the wall.

After listening carefully, Vivian had recommended to Becky that they set up the business on *QuickBooks*, a popular computerized bookkeeping program for small businesses. Joe and Becky already had a computer, but it wasn't being used for much except for some browsing on the Internet. Vivian determined that it was powerful enough to run *QuickBooks*.

Becky agreed that *QuickBooks* sounded great, so Vivian was currently working on downloading it from the Internet and customizing it to Joe and Becky's needs. Vivian had already set up the chart of accounts and was customizing the invoices with Joe's Plumbing information.

The stack of file folders was now filed in the filing cabinet and was sorted by month rather than by expense type. Each month's file now contained copies of all the Joe's Plumbing invoices, check stubs, expense receipts, and the bank statement for that month. Vivian was coming back tomorrow to start training Becky on how to use the system and how to reconcile her bank account.

For the first time since she and Joe started the business, Becky felt that she might not be drowning in paperwork after all. She sipped her coffee and smiled at Vivian.

Chapter Summary

- Setting up your record-keeping system properly from the beginning will, over the long term, save you an immense amount of time and money.
- Source documents must be kept for many years for taxation purposes.
- All of your company's financial transactions are recorded in a journal, which posts to account balances in a general ledger.
- Consider investing in a computerized accounting software program right from the start.

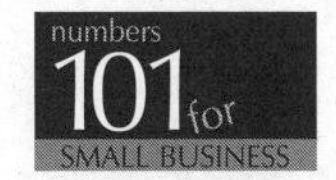

Chapter 5

The Balance Sheet

In this chapter, you will learn —

- The purpose of the balance sheet
- The accounts that make up the balance sheet
- How to value and present balance sheet items
- How to account for changes in the balance sheet

The balance sheet, from my perspective, gives the most grief to people, including small-business owners, bankers, and even bookkeepers.

What's so difficult about it? Each item on the balance sheet has its own rules (remember GAAP from Chapter 3?) as to how it must be valued and presented. Most items are generally valued at historical cost — that is, the cost at which the item was originally purchased. However, other valuation measures exist on the balance sheet including amortized cost, lower cost or market, and present value of future cash flows.

This chapter looks at the major assets, liabilities, and equity items on the balance sheet and discusses what they are and how they must be recorded.

The Purpose of the Balance Sheet

If you have read Chapters 1 and 2, you'll recall that the two main purposes of bookkeeping are to record a company's net worth and to record the results of its financial transactions over a period.

The balance sheet is a snapshot in time of everything a company owns and everything it owes at a particular moment. The things the company owns are called assets. The things it owes are called liabilities (when they are owed to outside parties) and equity (when they are owed to the owners of the

CASE STUDY

Vivian tried to recreate the balance sheet for Joe's Plumbing while Becky watched. Becky was concerned. She had never tried to track the assets and liabilities for the company before. She thought she needed only to add up the income and expenses at the end of the year for the tax return.

Vivian had explained that it was important to keep an eye on the balance sheet. It was like a road map that could tell Joe and Becky where they were headed and if they were going to veer off the road. She found all the current accounts receivable, accounts payable, and bank and inventory balances and put them into *QuickBooks* as opening balances. Becky had the bank fax over loan statements to get a current balance on the loan.

Vivian explained that the business had more assets than liabilities, and that the difference between the two was Joe and Becky's equity in the company, some of which had originally come from Joe putting personal funds into the company, and some of which had come from the accumulated income over the years in the business. Vivian set up the equity accounts and showed Becky how to find the balance sheet report in the system.

business). Sample 3 shows a typical balance sheet.

Notice that the total assets and the total liabilities and equity balance; that is to say, debits equal credits. Because assets have debit balances and liabilities and owner's equity have credit balances, we can also say that:

ASSETS = LIABILITIES + OWNER'S EQUITY

This is called the fundamental accounting equation. Although the concept itself is important to learn, the name is not.

You will find that every balance sheet (and this goes for all of the financial statements) will look a little different. Some accountants prefer not to use any dollar signs. Some like to have assets on one page and liabilities on the next. Regardless of how it looks, though, the fundamental accounting equation still holds.

The Components of the Balance Sheet

What follows is a look at the various components that may make up the balance sheet.

Assets

Assets represent what a company owns. Assets are usually broken down into three categories:

- **Current assets:** These are assets that can be easily converted into the most liquid and readily tradable asset of all — cash — within 12 months.
- **Capital assets:** These are assets that provide the company with operating capability. They are more permanent in nature than are current assets and will have value for many years. Some common examples are machinery, computer equipment, furniture and fixtures, and land and buildings.
- **Other assets:** These are assets that cannot be defined as either current or capital. There are very few assets that belong in this category, the most notable of which are incorporation costs and goodwill.

Let's look at each of the main assets you may have on your balance sheet. Assets are usually listed on the balance sheet in liquidity

Sample 3
BALANCE SHEET

Small Company Inc.
Balance Sheet
31 December 2003

Assets		
	Current	
	Bank	$1,259
	Accounts receivable	14,908
	Inventory	8,475
		24,642
	Capital assets	**137,412**
	Other assets	**989**
	Total assets	**$163,043**
Liabilities		
	Current	
	Accounts payable	$21,071
	Government remittances	2,221
	Income taxes	952
	Due to shareholder	17,549
		41,793
	Long Term	
	Mortgage payable	81,562
		123,355
Shareholders' Equity		
	Retained earnings	$39,678
	Capital stock	10
	Total liabilities and equity	**$163,043**

order, which means you start the list with those assets that you can most readily convert into cash.

Petty cash

Petty cash is the amount of money you have on hand. Most companies have a box containing small amounts of cash for small purchases like stamps, cream for coffee, and courier charges. (For more information on how to run a petty cash system, see Chapter 15.) The amount of money physically in the box should equal the balance of the petty cash account on the balance sheet.

Bank

This line on your balance sheet represents the amount of money you have in the company's bank account. At the end of every month, you will reconcile this account from the bank statements. (Chapter 16 looks at the reconciliation process.) Because there may be items that have been posted in the books that have not yet cleared the bank, the balance may not exactly equal what's on your bank statement. The reconciliation process will help you determine if your balance is correct.

Accounts receivable

Accounts receivable is the amount that your customers owe you in total. If you do not sell goods or services on credit, you will not have accounts receivable. You — or your accounting program — will usually keep a sub-ledger detailing who owes you and how old that account is. The balance sheet figure is only a summary.

Allowance for doubtful accounts (AFDA)

This is a sub-section of accounts receivable. It is called a contra account, because it goes against (or nets off) the receivables. The AFDA represents a reserve for those accounts receivable that you think you might not be able to collect. If you are sure that an account is a bad debt, you would simply remove it from the accounts receivable all together. However, if you have some accounts that you think but don't know for sure are uncollectible, you would credit this account and debit bad debts expense on the income statement. Notice that putting something in AFDA brings down the balance of the accounts receivable. That makes intuitive sense, as you do not think that these accounts are, in fact, collectible.

Inventory

Your inventory is the goods that you purchase to resell (if you are a retailer) or goods that you are in the process of constructing for sale (if you are a manufacturer). In addition, some service industries have time inventory. (For more information, see Chapter 10.) Inventory is an asset to you because you will eventually get benefit from it later, as you will receive cash when you sell it.

Inventory is usually recorded in the books at its cost to you. In the case of a manufacturer, this amount is the cost of all of the component parts plus the cost of labor and overhead attributable to those items that are in the process of construction and not yet sold.

In certain industries, inventory can be recorded at different costs. However, a discussion of those methods is beyond the scope of this book.

Prepaid expenses

These are expenses that the company has already paid but which relate to a period in the future. They are assets because the company will receive value next year from having already paid that amount this year. A common example of a prepaid expense is business insurance. If your company's year end is December 31 and you pay your renewal on your insurance policy on November 1 for the period November 1 to the following October 31, much of that insurance expense belongs in the next year.

To account for the prepaid portion, you would multiply the total insurance payment by the amount of time that belongs in the next period and set that up as an asset. In the above example, if the insurance payment was $1,000, the prepaid portion would be —

$1,000 X 304/365 = $832.88 prepaid

The balance of the payment (that is, $167.12) would be put in the insurance expense category in the general journal.

Capital assets

You may be more familiar with the older term "Fixed Assets." As mentioned above, these are assets that have long-term value to the company, and provide your business with the capacity to operate.

Capital assets are initially recorded at their cost to purchase. If there are additional costs — such as installation costs for equipment or legal fees on a land purchase — these are included in the cost of the asset and not expensed separately, as they are an integral part of the asset. Each period, **depreciation** (also called **amortization**) is taken on the undepreciated balance of the asset. Depreciation recognizes that most capital assets are worth less over time and that the value assigned to a capital asset should correspondingly decline. Each type of asset gets depreciated at a different rate; some are straight line (meaning that the same amount is depreciated each period); some are declining balance (meaning that a percentage of the remaining undepreciated balance is depreciated every period). Here are some examples:

Manufacturing equipment purchased for $1,250 — 30 percent declining balance means —

1) Initial entry:

DR	**Equipment**	**$1,250.00**
CR	**Cash (or Accounts payable)**	**$1,250.00**

2) Depreciation entry end of year:

DR	**Depreciation expense (30% X $1,250)**	**$375.00**
CR	**Accumulated depreciation — equipment**	**$375.00**

In the next year, depreciation would be 30 percent of the remaining undepreciated balance (that is, $875) or $262.50.

The accumulated depreciation account is a contra account: it nets the equipment account balance downward. Therefore, the net of the equipment account and the accumulated depreciation account is meant to be an approximation of the worth of the asset. Of course, it will never perfectly reflect the fair market value of the asset. As depreciation rates and methods differ between asset types and between countries, you should talk to your accountant about the capital assets on your balance sheet.

Other assets

Goodwill

Goodwill is a difficult concept to understand, even for accountants. So much so, in fact, that generally accepted accounting principles in many countries are in the process of changing because of it.

When we speak of goodwill, we refer to that part of a business that is unrelated to its hard assets. Rather, goodwill refers to the fact that customers know the business name and keep coming back. In general, goodwill is assigned a value on the balance sheet only when it is purchased.

For example, if you run a machine repair shop, and it buys out one of its competitors for $30,000, some of that purchase price will relate to the equipment and other assets you purchased, but some might relate to the fact that the competitor had loyal customers that are expected to remain with you. This portion of the purchase price would be the goodwill.

Goodwill falls into the category of other assets. However, the variety of methods of valuing goodwill and amortizing it are beyond the scope of this book.

Incorporation costs

When a company incorporates, there are costs involved, including registration costs and, sometimes, legal fees. These costs do not relate to any particular operating period. They encompass the entire life of the company. Therefore, these incorporation costs are capitalized (i.e., set up as an asset on the balance sheet). These costs are amortized over time (usually ten years) to slowly expense them over that period.

Liabilities

Liabilities represent what the company owes. They are usually broken down on the balance sheet into two categories:

- **Current liabilities:** Those that are expected to be paid in the next 12 months
- **Long-term liabilities:** Those that will not be paid in the next 12 months

What follows is a look at the most common types of liabilities.

Current liabilities

Bank indebtedness

If your company has an overdraft or an operating line of credit that is due on demand by the bank, it will fall into this category. It will not include loans with fixed repayment terms. (These are discussed below.)

When you make purchases against your line of credit, the accounting is almost identical to the way it would be if you were buying the item with a positive cash balance. The only difference is that bank indebtedness carries a credit balance instead of the debit balance of a cash account.

Accounts payable

These are amounts that you owe to your suppliers for products and services they have sold to you on credit. There is usually an accounts payable sub-ledger that shows the details of which supplier is owed and how old that debt is.

Accrued liabilities

These are amounts that you owe suppliers but for which they have not yet billed you. Accrued liabilities are usually accounted for only at the end of the year when your accountant prepares your financial statements. It relates to the matching principle mentioned earlier in the chapter. The purpose of setting up the accrued liabilities is to get the expenses into the proper period, the one in which the expense was "consumed."

One of the most common accrued liabilities is the accountant's fee. It makes sense that the fee should be included in the year in which it relates; but for obvious reasons, the accountant has not yet billed you for preparation of the year end. He or she would therefore make the following entry:

DR Professional fees (an expense) $XXX
CR Accrued liabilities $XXX

This entry would be reversed in the next year as the actual expense is processed through accounts payable.

Government remittances payable

This category can encompass many items, depending on where you do business. In the US, it would include mainly payroll remittances and state sales taxes. In Canada, it would include GST, PST, HST, and payroll remittances. In Britain, it includes the VAT.

The common element among all the items placed in this category is that these are amounts that are collected from customers or employees on behalf of one of the levels of government. You can think of government remittances payable as a trust account: You are holding these amounts in trust for the government. When you collect the taxes from customers or employees, you credit this account; and when you remit them to the government, you debit the account for the amount of the payment. Therefore, the balance in this account should reflect only those amounts that have been collected but not yet remitted.

Income taxes payable

Income taxes payable applies only if your business is incorporated. If it is a sole proprietorship or partnership, the income taxes payable are those of the owners, not the business itself. Only corporations are regarded by the government as being separate legal entities from their owners, and therefore liable for filing their own income tax returns.

This account tracks the balances owing to the various levels of government (federal, state, provincial) that levy income taxes on the corporation. At the end of every year, you will calculate your income tax liability and post it into the books like this:

DR Income tax expense $XXX
CR Income taxes payable $XXX

When you pay the amount owing, you will debit the income tax payable account and credit the bank.

During the year, you may be required to prepay income taxes by paying installments to the government. You would record these transactions like this:

DR Income taxes payable $XXX
CR Bank $XXX

It is therefore possible to have a debit balance in the income taxes payable account.

Due to/from shareholders

This account will only exist for incorporated businesses. It tracks the amounts owing to and from the shareholders of the company. These amounts are different from the longer-term capital contributions of the shareholders that appear in the equity section.

Two main types of transactions can occur to generate amounts owing to and from the shareholders: when the company pays for a personal expense of the shareholder, and when the shareholder pays for a business expense out of his or her own pocket. (See Chapter 13 for an in-depth look at these types of transactions.)

Long-term liabilities

The most common long-term liabilities will, of course, include your company's mortgage.

Mortgage payable

If the company owns the building in which it operates and carries a mortgage against it, you will record the liability for the mortgage in this category on the balance sheet. The mortgage is originally recorded like this:

DR Building	**$XXX**	
CR Bank (for deposit)		**$XXX**
CR Mortgage payable		**XXX**

When mortgage payments are made, they are usually a combination of interest and principal. A payment would be recorded like this:

DR Mortgage payable (for principal portion)	**$XXX**	
DR Interest expense (for interest portion)	**XXX**	
CR Bank (for entire payment)		**$XXX**

Frequently, small businesses — for ease of bookkeeping — apply the entire payment to either interest or mortgage payable, and the accountant adjusts the mortgage balance at the end of the year to correspond with the mortgage statements from the lender. Although this method is easier, it creates a misrepresentation on your balance sheet until it is corrected.

Equity

The third section of the balance sheet is the equity section. This section of your balance sheet may look a little different from that in Sample 3, depending on your form of business ownership.

Let's look at the main components of the equity section for a corporation.

Capital stock

Capital stock exists only in a corporation. It represents the shareholders' ownership of the business. In most countries, the capital stock appears only on the balance sheet at a nominal cost, meaning that the shares are not meant to represent their market value; they're meant only to be place holders so that readers of the financial statements can tell that they exist.

In the corporation's incorporation documents, there will be a statement of the nominal value of each share. For example, if you are the only shareholder and you have subscribed for 100 shares at $0.01 per share, the value of the shares on the balance sheet would be 100 X $0.01, or $1.00. You would give the company $1 cash, and it would issue 100 shares to you from its treasury.

There may be different classes of capital stock outstanding in your corporation:

Common stock: This kind of stock is usually (but not always) the only voting stock issued, making common stockholders the true owners of the business. Holders of common stock get to vote on issues such as the payment of dividends, the appointment of directors, and the signing of significant trade contracts.

Preferred stock: Preferred stock is sometimes called preference or "pref" shares and is a different class of shares from common stock. There may be several series of these shares (Pref A, Pref B, etc.). They are called preferred because, in the event of the liquidation of the corporation, preferred stock holders will receive the value coming to them from the corporation before (or in preference to) the common shareholders. Preferred shares are also frequently used in tax and estate planning for small corporations, subjects that are beyond the scope of this book.

Capital contributions

You may need to include a line on your balance sheet for capital contributions. This category is also a corporate account and represents any amounts that the shareholders of the company invest in the business on a semi-permanent basis. For example, if a shareholder knows that the company will need financing to cover its accounts receivable, the shareholder may invest $20,000 in the corporation and not expect it back in the short term. If the shareholder does expect it to be returned soon, you would post it to the due to/from shareholder category in the liabilities section.

Retained earnings

Retained earnings represent the accumulated amount of income the corporation still possesses after it has paid all taxes and dividends (discussed below). This net income has accumulated over the life of the corporation. Here's an example:

Yr 1	Net income	$1,000
	Less: Income taxes	(250)
	Less: Dividends paid	(425)
	Equals: Retained earnings	$325

Yr 2	Net income	$1,200
	Less: Income taxes	(300)
	Less: Dividends paid	(150)
	Plus: Opening retained earnings	325
	Equals: Closing retained earnings	$1,075

Dividends

Dividends are payments to the shareholders to compensate them for their ownership in the corporation. It is the same concept as utilized in large corporations. If you invested in the stock market (in IBM, let's say), you would receive a quarterly dividend check from IBM as payment on your shareholdings. When you are the shareholder of a small corporation, the same logic holds.

Dividends are a part of the equity section of the balance sheet because they are drawn out of the corporation's after-tax retained earnings. They do not represent a deduction to the company on its income statement. The year after the dividend has been declared and paid, it is merged into the retained earnings of the company, so that only the current year dividends appear separately in this column.

A sole proprietorship's equity section will look a little different from a corporation's. There are no shares, retained earnings, or contributed capital. There is only one account: Owner's Equity. There can, however, be a few sub-sections of owner's equity, but usually only the summary figure appears on the balance sheet. Here are the components:

CASE STUDY

After Vivian left for the day, Becky printed off her very first balance sheet from *QuickBooks*. She found it comforting to be able to see all of the assets and liabilities in one place. She felt more in control of the numbers.

Vivian had shown Becky how to compare her current assets to her current liabilities to make sure that the company stayed solvent. Becky knew now that they had $1.12 in assets for every $1.00 of liabilities. Although cash was tight, they should be able to get by for the next 12 months.

Becky printed another copy of the balance sheet and put it in Joe's in basket for him to see when he got home. Was he ever going to be surprised!

Accumulated earnings: The concept of accumulated earnings is similar to that of retained earnings, above, but because an unincorporated business has no income taxes of its own or dividends to pay out, it is truly an accumulation of the income of the business for all the years it has been in existence.

Proprietor's (or partners') draws: This line represents the accumulation of money that the proprietor (or partner, in a partnership) has drawn out of the business over time. It represents funds no longer in the company. In a way, it's a little like corporate dividends in that it is withdrawals of capital, but the tax treatment of these items is completely different. (As always, talk to your accountant about taxation issues.)

Proprietor's (or partners') contributions: This represents the accumulation of money that the proprietor (or partner, in a partnership) has invested in the company.

You can see by the nature of these equity items that net income and contributions would increase the net equity account, and net losses and draws would decrease it. It's also important to note that the only difference between the equity section for a partnership and the equity section for a sole proprietorship is that in a partnership, the equity section would show each partner's draws and contributions and the net income would be split between the partners according to their ownership. Even though only the summary figure would go on the balance sheet, an equity ledger would be maintained to track each partner's equity. Sample 4 shows an equity statement for a partnership.

Note that the partner draws and contributions relate to each individual partner. The net income for the year is split among partners based on their share of ownership in the partnership. In the example below, the partners are 50/50 owners, and each receives half of the income.

Sample 4

PARTNERSHIP EQUITY STATEMENT

	John Mason	Sandra Peck	Total
Opening partners'equity	$47,912	$53,967	$101,879
Net income for year	12,460	12,460	24,920
Partner draws	(10,000)	(9,750)	(19,750)
Partner contributions	1,000	0	1,000
Ending partners'equity	$51,372	$56,677	$108,049

Chapter Summary

- The balance sheet represents a snapshot of what a company owns and owes at a given moment.
- Most items on the balance sheet are recorded at their original or historical cost, but there are some exceptions.
- Current assets will be converted to cash within 12 months and current liabilities will be paid within the next 12 months.
- Retained earnings represents the income a company has accumulated over its lifetime but which hasn't yet been distributed to the owners.

Chapter 6

The Income Statement

In this chapter, you will learn —

- The purpose of an income statement
- How the income statement corresponds to the balance sheet
- What the major components of an income statement are and how to record the data
- What happens if you have more expenses than revenue

The income statement probably gets more attention than the other two major financial statements — the balance sheet and the cash flow statement — and probably more attention than it deserves. It shows the net income (or net profit, as it is also called), which represents revenues minus expenses, but doesn't show much about the stability of the business.

Think of it this way: The income statement shows the top edge of a house being built. It shows the new bricks and mortar being laid on, piece by piece. The faster the bricks are being laid and the more plentiful they are, the happier the homeowner is.

The balance sheet is the foundation. It displays the result of all of the previous brick laying. It doesn't matter how fast the new bricks are going in. If there are gaps (or gaaps — a little accounting humor!) in the foundation or if the house wobbles from the quality of the brickwork, the house will fall.

The Purpose of the Income Statement

The income statement is a summary of a company's income-producing activities over a specific period. Remember that the balance sheet is a snapshot of a particular moment. The income statement shows what happened in the period leading up to that moment. Sample 5 shows a typical income statement.

Income statements are also sometimes called the statement of profit and loss (or the

CASE STUDY

Becky flipped through the Joe's Plumbing invoices they had billed out the prior year. This was the first time she had really examined them after the customers had paid. Vivian had asked her to try to separate the invoices into the type of work that was done. Becky had identified four major categories: subcontract work, commercial new installation, residential new installation, and residential repair.

Becky separated the piles of invoices into four stacks and added up each category. Vivian showed her how to enter that information into the historical performance area of the software so that she could compare the current year to the last year to see how they were doing.

Becky saw the benefit right away. Joe had been complaining for months that he felt that the residential new installation work was dropping off. He seemed to be going out on fewer jobs of that type. Until now, however, they had no way of tracking that information to see if it were true. Becky had simply added up all the receipts at the end of the year to put on the tax returns.

P&L). Although there will be some minor changes in presentation, income statements all have some things in common:

- *Revenue:* This number is always presented at the top, before any expenses.
- *Cost of goods sold (COGS):* This expense is always shown next. COGS is the cost of the products that were sold during the period (i.e., the items for which you received the revenue). If a company sells services instead of goods, there will be no cost of goods sold line.
- *Gross margin:* The total for the gross margin line will equal revenue minus cost of goods sold. In all cases, the gross margin should be a positive number, because it reflects only the cost of the product you sell. For example, if you sold 100 gadgets at $4.75 each, for which you paid $2.15, your revenue would be $475, and your cost of goods sold would be $215, leaving you with a gross margin of $260. The only way that the gross margin would be negative would be if you were selling goods for less than your cost to purchase or manufacture them. You wouldn't stay in business very long doing that!
- *Expenses:* Some income statements do not categorize expenses, but those that do usually separate them into sales, administrative, and general expenses. Sales expenses are those costs directly related to the sales process: your marketing manager's salary, advertising, and promotion. Administrative expenses would include the costs of your premises (rent), receptionist's salary, office supplies, and anything else necessary to your "back office" operations. The general expenses category is the catchall basin for everything else.
- *Earnings before income tax (EBIT):* EBIT will be the figure you are left with once you total your expenses, then deduct them from your gross margin. EBIT shows your total net profit

Sample 5
STATEMENT OF INCOME

Small Company Inc.
Statement of Income
For the Year Ended 31 December 2003

Revenue	$247,912
Cost of goods sold	83,503
Gross margin	164,409
Expenses	
Advertising	1,257
Bank charges	410
Depreciation	9,340
Meals & entertainment	953
Office expenses	4,459
Professional fees	1,650
Supplies	7,285
Telephone & utilities	2,671
Vehicle expenses	6,692
Wages	37,942
	72,659
Earnings before income taxes	91,750
Income taxes	22,938
Net income	**$68,812**

before your income tax expense for the period it is calculated. However, the EBIT number may be different than the number that you are taxed on in your income tax returns for a number of reasons (a discussion of which is beyond the scope of this book). If a company is not incorporated, there will be no EBIT, because there will be no income taxes shown. An unincorporated company is not subject to its own taxes; rather its owners are taxed on the company's earnings as part of their personal taxes.

- *Income taxes:* As discussed above, this figure will appear only on a corporation's income statement. The income tax expense represents the tax expense related to the current period (listed at the top of the income statement). It may or may not be different from the income tax payable number on the balance sheet.

An income statement can have many different components, which will be discussed further in this chapter.

What's on My Income Statement?

Your income statement shows you several "layers" of information. You may have two or more income statements: a summary statement for the external users, and a more detailed, longer version for internal management purposes. On the one hand, as a manager, you most likely want to see your profit product-by-product, to know which of your lines are really making you money. An external income statement, on the other hand, will most likely show revenue as a single line item, perhaps with a schedule attached to the income statement showing revenue from each source, but rarely the profit each source generates.

Earlier, I described the various items you will find on the income statement. Now it's time to group them.

The first grouping on your income statement gives you the results from ongoing operations. It is this part of the income statement that is shown in Sample 5.

Ongoing operations means the regular, day-to-day business that your company does. If no events have occurred outside this category, your income statement ends here.

However, there are myriad financial events that, although they happened and therefore must be recorded in your books, nonetheless are unusual and aren't expected to happen again. These are called extraordinary items, and most accounting rules require that these items be shown separately on the income statement.

The reason for this becomes clear if you think about it from an investor's perspective. For example, if you were trying to decide whether or not to invest money in a corporation that is showing a net income of $775,000, you would want to know what that includes. If half of it resulted from a gain on sale of most of that company's equipment, you would then know two things. First, there is $387,500 of net income that will never happen again. Second, the company sold most of its equipment, so how is it going to produce any income in the future? This is why accounting rules in most countries require that these extraordinary gains and losses be shown separately on the income statement. Doing so highlights unusual financial events in a company's books.

Below are some examples of extraordinary events that may need to be separated out on your income statement. (**Note:** Different countries have different rules regarding which items must be broken out like this and which are simply a part of ongoing operations. Check with your accountant if you have any questions.)

Proceeds or payments from lawsuits: If your company has to pay out money as a result of a lawsuit or receives a settlement of claim, obviously (you hope!) this type of expense or revenue would not happen again.

Change in your accounting methods: Remember earlier when we talked about the fact that there are acceptable alternatives in choosing accounting methods? Changing from one method to another can have a large impact on your company's current year revenue as a result of "catching up" with the new method. This is a one-time occurrence that should be shown separately.

Business restructuring: The format of your business could change dramatically. If you abandon a segment of your business or lay off many of your employees, financial statement readers will need to know that these expenses will not recur regularly. The expenses of abandoning a segment of your business may include the loss on sale of equipment or extra staff wages for the transfer of assets. Expenses of laying off employees may include severance or early retirement packages, or the unusually large payout of vacation pay.

Asset write-downs: These could come from several sources. Inventory may be written down to its net recoverable value or written off completely if it has no value. Loans that the company has made to others might go bad and require writing off. Equipment might be lost in a factory fire. All these things would necessitate an adjustment to the income statement and would be shown as extraordinary items.

Each extraordinary item must be shown separately on the income statement after the net income from continuing operations line. Each extraordinary item line is actually a summary number from a mini-income statement. For example, obtaining a legal settlement of claim might involve the following income and expense items:

Proceeds received from settlement	$74,000
Less: legal fees paid to lawyer	(32,412)
Less: court costs	(1,692)
Less: registered mail costs	(157)
Net proceeds of settlement before taxes	**39,739**
Income tax expense on settlement	(9,934)
Net proceeds of settlement	**$29,805**

Note that this mini-income statement would show on the income statement of the company as follows:

Net proceeds of settlement net of taxes	$29,805

Breaking out the income and expenses of extraordinary items allows you to look at each individual item and understand all the income or expense items that are connected to that event.

Interpreting the Income Statement

How do you read the income statement? How do you know what it's telling you?

The income statement is like a history book, presenting to you the story of what's happened to your business over a specific period. That period will be shown near the top of the statement, where you'll place the phrase, "For the year ended XXX," or something similar. This phrase allows you to quickly identify in which period the revenues and expenses occurred.

You'll find that reviewing income statements is most useful when you look at more than one period together, so that you can see each period in relation to others. It's one thing to know that you had net income of $50,000 this year, but it makes a difference whether last year you made $25,000 or $110,000. It's

CASE STUDY

Now that Becky had separated the Joe's Plumbing invoices into the four major categories, she could see right away that month-by-month compared to last year, the residential new installation work was dwindling. She also saw that the subcontract work was really taking off. It wasn't that business was down; they were just refocusing their efforts.

Vivian had set up the revenue accounts for the new year using the four categories that Becky had identified. From now on, they would be able to see at the push of a button how they were doing in each of the four areas.

Vivian also set up four cost of sales accounts that correlated to the revenue accounts. This way, she had explained, all the direct costs related to those types of sales would be matched with the revenues, allowing Joe and Becky to see which type of work was the most profitable.

"The more information you have about the past, the better management decisions you can make about the future," Vivian had said. Becky knew that this was finally the beginning of getting control over their business.

the trend you're interested in here. In what direction is the net income heading?

Here are some issues to address when looking at the income statement:

Is your gross margin the same as last year? If it's lower, it could mean that you're selling more goods than last year but at a lower profit margin. This would be your signal to examine your sales and supply practices more closely. If your gross margin is higher, you need to understand why. Did you find a new supplier this year who sold you your materials for production at a lower cost? You may have permanent savings from such an accomplishment. Did you substitute cheaper-quality goods for your usual goods? If so, you will want to make sure your revenues are just as high as always and that you are not facing major customer dissatisfaction.

Are your administration expenses growing? If you moved into larger premises in the current year, you need to make sure that the move is producing the results you were expecting. For example, if by moving to your new showroom right on the highway you expected to increase revenues by 20 percent, did that increase occur? Measure the results by looking at the increase in revenues since the date of the move compared to the same time frame the previous year.

Have the revenues from your main product line decreased dramatically this year? If the answer to this question is yes, you must find the cause. Has a newer product come onto the market, taking a bite out of your sales? Has demand for your product declined in general, either through changing consumer tastes or swings in the economy? You must hunt down the underlying reasons for the change.

You can see that the income statement will, if you let it, provide you with valuable information to help you run your business. Much like the reflectors on a dark highway, it can show you where the road is and warn you when you're going to veer off. However, I will once again caution you that it's also important to look at all three financial statements together — the income statement, balance sheet (discussed in the previous chapter), and cash flow (discussed in the next chapter). They each provide a different piece of the story, and their interrelation provides the subplot.

The Statement of Retained Earnings: A Tag-Along

There is actually a fourth financial statement that bears discussion: the statement of retained earnings. This document is a reconciliation of the changes to the retained earnings account. It can be presented in many ways, but the most common is to append it to the bottom of the income statement. Sample 6 shows a statement of retained earnings such as may be appended to the bottom of an income statement.

This statement starts with the closing retained earnings from the prior year (which becomes the opening retained earnings for the current year), then adds the net income after taxes for the year (or deducts the net loss), and deducts any dividends paid to the shareholders. Remember that dividends come out of retained earnings; that's why they appear here and not as an expense on the income statement.

Sample 6
STATEMENT OF RETAINED EARNINGS

Small Company Inc.
Statement of Retained Earnings
For the Year Ended 31 December 2003

Opening retained earnings	$11,573
Net income for the year	68,812
Dividends	(40,707)
Closing retained earnings	$39,678

Chapter Summary

- The income statement shows the results of operations for a specific period, but doesn't provide information on the stability of the business.
- The income statement is split between the results of regular operations and extraordinary financial events.
- Looking at the income statement for more than a single period provides the most information about the direction of the business.
- The statement of retained earnings is usually shown at the bottom of the income statement and shows the cumulative net equity position of the owners of the business.

The Cash Flow Statement

In this chapter, you will learn —

- The connection between the cash flow statement and the other two major financial statements
- The purpose of the cash flow statement
- The main components of the cash flow statement
- How to prepare the cash flow statement

The cash flow statement has always been the country cousin of the other two major financial statements. Misunderstood and confusing, it can be difficult for small-business owners to interpret and use.

However, the cash flow statement tells the story every business owner wants to hear: "Where did my money go?" It's the only statement of the three that deals in cash inflows and outflows. For example, if your cash balance was $15,000 at the end of last year and it's $12,000 at the end of this year, you know that you had net cash outflows of $3,000 for the year. But where did it go? How did it get there? The cash flow statement reconciles your opening cash to your closing cash for the period. This chapter examines what the cash flow statement can tell you and give you the details on how to prepare one for your business.

Categorizing Cash Flows

Your cash inflows and outflows over the course of the year could come from many sources. Some examples are the following:

- Net income for the year
- Sale of equipment
- Owner contribution
- Purchase of assets
- Dividend payments

CASE STUDY

"What's really bothering us is that we can't seem to get ahead." Becky leaned forward in her chair as she spoke on the phone with Vivian. "It's great that I can now see what we own and what we owe on the balance sheet, and I already know we're making money. There's always income at the end of the year that we get taxed on. But there never seems to be any money in the bank account. Is there a report in the accounting software that can tell me where all our money is going?"

Vivian could hear the frustration in Becky's voice. She had heard it in the voices of hundreds of small-business owners who didn't have a good handle on the inflows and outflows of cash in their business. They didn't understand how changes in accounts receivable, accounts payable, and inventory affected cash levels.

"Becky," she started soothingly, "now that you have your books computerized and organized, there's one more major financial statement that I need to show you how to prepare. It's called the cash flow statement. It will help you understand where your money is going."

- Loan proceeds
- Loan repayments
- Sale of marketable securities

The list goes on and on. It's useful to group these cash flows into types to give the list some structure.

There are three main types of cash flows:

Cash flow from operating activities: These include cash inflows from revenues and cash outflows from expenses. These are the flows of money that occur because of the day-to-day operations of your business.

Cash flow from investing activities: These include cash outflows from investing in new assets and cash inflows from selling off old assets. Assets can include land and buildings, equipment, furniture, or marketable securities.

Cash flow from financing activities: These include cash inflows from borrowing funds or from new injections of capital from the shareholders and cash outflows from the repayment of loans as well as the payment of capital or dividends to the shareholders of the corporation.

Now that you know how to classify your cash flows, how do you calculate them?

Back to the Balance Sheet: The Basis of the Cash Flow Statement

Think of cash flow this way: each inflow and outflow makes a change on the balance sheet. Even inflows from net income increase retained earnings. Really, all the cash flow statement does is show you the change in each of the balance sheet accounts, including the cash account.

Sample 7 shows a comparative balance sheet for the years ended December 31, 2002 and 2003, using the same financial information as used in the previous two chapters.

You can see that the cash (as shown in the bank line) decreased from $10,295 at the end of the first year to $1,259 at the end of

Sample 7
COMPARATIVE BALANCE SHEET

Small Company Inc.
Balance Sheet
31 December 2003

		2003	2002
Assets			
	Current		
	Bank	$1,259	$10,295
	Accounts receivable	14,908	9,640
	Inventory	8,475	3,725
		24,642	**23,660**
	Capital assets	137,412	145,219
	Other assets	989	1,047
	Total assets	**$163,043**	**$169,926**
Liabilities			
	Current		
	Accounts payable	$21,071	$47,816
	Government remittances	2,221	1,758
	Income taxes	952	875
	Due to shareholder	17,549	12,419
		41,793	**62,868**
	Long Term		
	Mortgage payable	81,562	95,475
		123,355	**158,343**
	Shareholders' equity		
	Retained earnings	39,678	11,573
	Capital stock	10	10
	Total liabilities and equity	**$163,043**	**$169,926**

CASE STUDY

"Even I can see what happened last year now," Joe said. "Look at the big increase in inventory and receivables. The inventory cost us money, and the accounts receivable balance going up means we didn't get that money in. That ends up costing us money too."

Becky studied the cash flow statement and frowned. "Oh, and I had forgotten that we paid off that big loan with the bank last year. That's one of the reasons it feels like money is tight."

Vivian smiled at both of them. "You're right. Those are three big reasons why your cash balance fell last year. When we have completed this year's transactions, we'll review the cash flow again and see what has changed. If the inventory and receivables levels are still a problem, we'll start mapping out a solution."

the second year. Therefore, you know that you need to account for the $9,036 reduction in cash. Look at Sample 8 (which, for illustration purposes, includes a column headed "Difference") to see what else changed on the balance sheet.

Each change in the balance sheet represents either a net source or use of cash. For example, your accounts payable decreased by $26,745, meaning that you had to find the cash to pay it down. It is a use of cash. However, your accounts receivable increased by $5,268. This means that you did not have that extra $5,268 in your bank account, because it has not been collected yet. It is also a use of cash.

There are a few things to keep in mind while preparing your cash flow statement:

Non-cash items: Because the cash flow statement is concerned only with cash inflows and outflows, you will want to make sure that you do not take into consideration any non-cash items that appear on the balance sheet. The major one is the change in retained earnings due to depreciation expense for the year. The actual cash flow from the capital asset happened when the asset was purchased. Depreciation only tries to bring that original cost into expenses over time. No cash changes hands. Depreciation, therefore, must be excluded from your cash flow statement. You do this by starting with the net income number and adding the depreciation expense back into it. Doing so gives you what the net income would have been if it didn't have any depreciation (but not the income on a cash basis — that comes from the calculation of cash flow from operating activities).

Capital assets: A related issue is the change in capital assets on the balance sheet. This change could include three things: increases in the account due to capital asset purchases, decreases due to capital asset sales, and depreciation expense for the current year. As explained above, you must exclude the depreciation from the calculation, as no cash changed hands. Your cash flow statement will include only purchases and disposals of capital assets.

Sample 8

BALANCE SHEET WITH DIFFERENCE

Small Company Inc.
Balance Sheet
31 December 2003

		2003	2002	Difference
Assets				
	Current			
	Bank	$1,259	$10,295	(9,036)
	Accounts receivable	14,908	9,640	5,268
	Inventory	8,475	3,725	4,750
		24,642	**23,660**	
	Capital assets	137,412	145,219	(7,807)
	Other assets	989	1,047	(58)
	Total assets	**$163,043**	**$169,926**	
Liabilities				
	Current			
	Accounts payable	$21,071	$47,816	(26,745)
	Government remittances	2,221	1,758	463
	Income taxes	952	875	77
	Due to shareholder	17,549	12,419	5,130
		41,793	**62,868**	
	Long Term			
	Mortgage payable	81,562	95,475	(13,913)
		123,355	**158,343**	
	Shareholders' equity			
	Retained earnings	39,678	11,573	28,105
	Capital stock	10	10	0
	Total liabilities and equity	**$163,043**	**$169,926**	

Retained earnings: Although your cash flow statement looks at the changes in the balance sheet accounts, you must handle the change in retained earnings in a different manner than changes in the other accounts. You'll remember from Chapter 6 that retained earnings increases by the net income after taxes for the year (or decreases by the net loss) and decreases by dividends paid to the shareholders. The format of the cash flow statement breaks these elements into two pieces: The net income (or loss) is considered to be cash flow from operating activities, and dividend payments are cash flow from financing activities.

Now you're ready to prepare your cash flow statement!

Putting It All Together

In theory, once you've accounted for all other balance sheet changes, the change in cash should plop out the bottom. In reality, it can sometimes be a little tricky getting your cash flow statement to work.

It's important to talk it through if it's not working. "There is an increase in capital assets; therefore, that's a use of cash," and similar explanations will help keep you focused.

Sample 9 shows the cash flow statement produced from the comparative balance sheet shown in Sample 7.

Notice that you calculate the change in the cash (i.e., the total increase or decrease) for the year and then add it to the opening cash to get the closing cash. This works by calculation, but remember to actually compare the closing cash to your cash (bank) balance on your balance sheet!

What Is the Cash Flow Statement Telling Me?

Why is it important to look at the changes in cash for the year?

If you are an outside investor, you have an interest in knowing where all the money went because you want to make sure that some of it will come back to you in the form of interest or dividends. If you are the manager of the business, you also need a recap of where all the money went. For example, if the cash balance went down by $14,000 and most of it was due to an increase in accounts receivable, you need to know why your accounts receivable increased. Did your business grow by leaps and bounds over the year, causing you to finance the increase in the accounts receivable base with internal cash flow? Or did your accounts receivable clerk quit part way through the year, and your new one isn't nearly as good at getting money in the door? Once again, it's not numbers for numbers' sake; it's the story the numbers are telling you.

Sample 9
CASH FLOW STATEMENT

Small Company Inc.
Balance Sheet
31 December 2003

Net income	$68,812
Add back: Depreciation	9,340
	78,152
Cash from operating activities	
Increase in Accounts receivable	(5,268)
Increase in Inventory	(4,750)
Decrease in Accounts payable	(26,745)
Increase in Government remittances	463
Increase in Income taxes	77
Increase in Due to shareholder	5,130
Decrease in Mortgage payable	(13,913)
	(45,006)
Cash from investing activities	
Purchase of Capital assets	(1,475)
	(1,475)
Cash from financing activities	
Dividends	(40,707)
	(40,707)
Total decrease in cash	(9,036)
Opening cash balance	10,295
Closing cash balance	**$1,259**

Chapter Summary

- ➡ The cash flow statement is the only one of the three main financial statements that is prepared on a cash basis.
- ➡ The cash flow statement answers the question, "Where did the money go?"
- ➡ Only cash items are included in the statement, so depreciation on capital assets must be added back into income.
- ➡ The cash flow statement tells the management of the company a story. The numbers can illustrate problems or opportunities in the business.

INTERMEDIATE TOPICS

Chapter

8

Recording the Sales Cycle

In this chapter, you will learn —

- The components of the sales cycle
- How to account for credit sales
- How to treat discounts
- How to manage the accounts receivable ledger
- How to minimize and account for bad debts

Prior chapters have examined the operating cycle of a business: the time it takes for a business to complete the cash circuit. A business has cash, buys (or makes) products to sell — or provides services — and gets paid for them, thereby converting cash to purchases to accounts receivable back into cash. Figure 1 is an illustration of this cycle.

The operating cycle is composed of two pieces: the sales cycle and the purchases cycle. In any business, these two necessarily overlap, but it's easier to understand each piece if we separate them.

This chapter looks at the sales cycle and how to account for it. The next chapter will discuss the purchases cycle.

What Makes up the Sales Cycle?

The sales cycle consists of a collection of activities:

- Recording cash sales
- Recording credit sales and setting up the accounts receivable transactions
- Recording cash receipts and subsequent reductions in accounts receivable
- Preparing invoices
- Preparing statements of account
- Analyzing bad debts
- Writing off bad debts

We'll walk through each of these activities in detail and look at the accounting behind them. Where relevant, we will first talk about what happens in "real life," and

Figure 1

THE OPERATING CYCLE

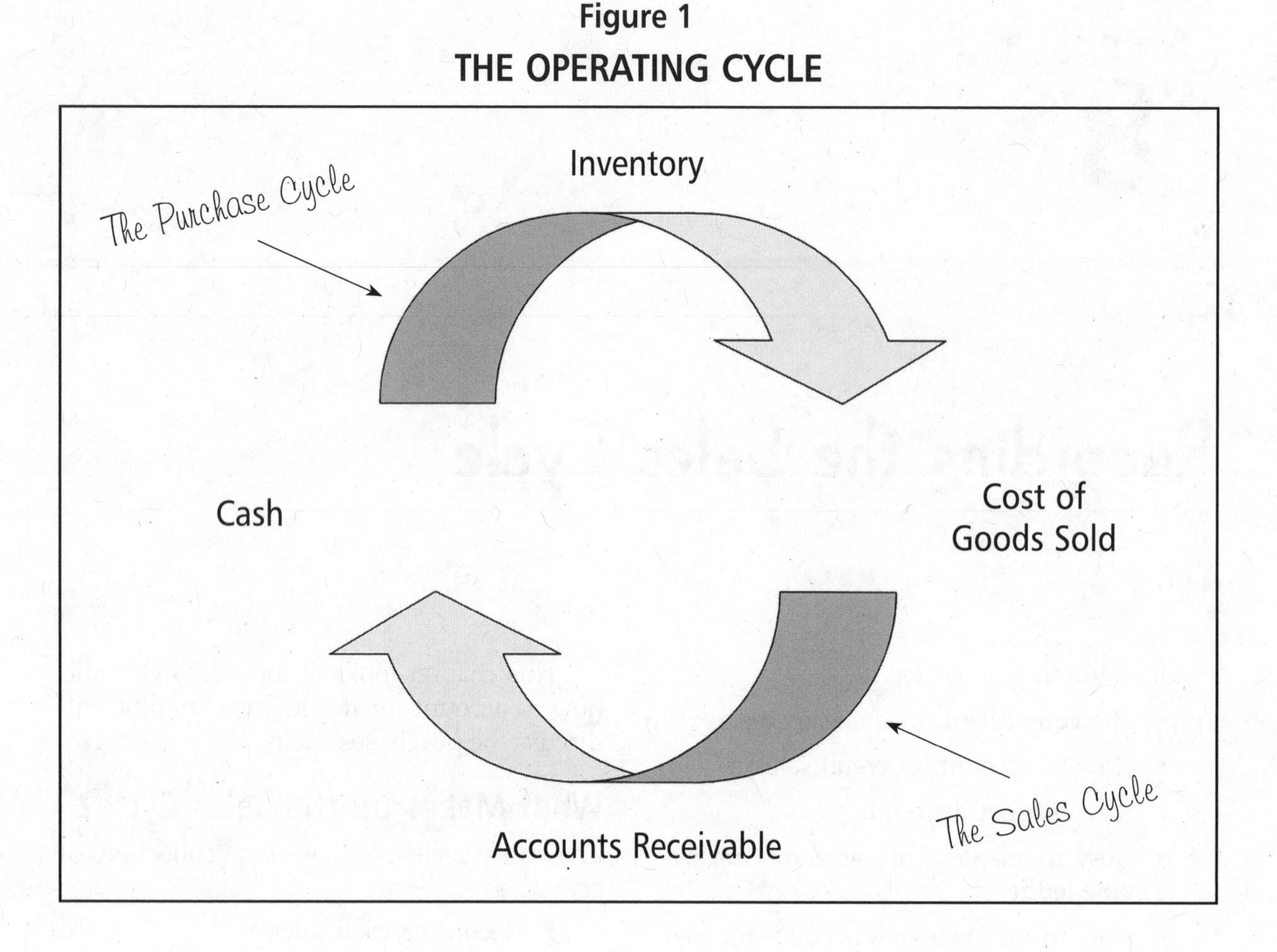

second, about what accounting you must do to mirror the transaction.

Recording Cash Sales

This is one of the easiest and most straightforward transactions.

Real life

A customer walks into your store, picks up a ceramic mug (assuming you sell ceramic mugs!), and brings it to the sales desk. You calculate the price, including taxes, and tell the customer how much it will cost all together. The customer hands you the money; you make change and record the transaction, either in the cash register or by using an invoice book (or computerized program). Whichever method you use to record the transaction, you will provide a copy of the receipt or invoice to the customer and will retain one for your records. If you are using a cash register, there will be an internal tape recording the transaction. If you use an invoice book, it should be at least a two-part

CASE STUDY

Becky knew the list of customers who owed Joe's Plumbing money would have to go. Vivian had entered all of the receivables into *QuickBooks*, so now Becky could see the list any time she liked. She still was hesitant to part with it, however. She had begun it when she and Joe had first started up the company. It comforted her to know that people still owed them money.

Vivian had a different take on the list. She noticed that some of the receivables were almost a year old. She had reviewed these with Becky and had looked at the account activity since then.

"These customers have paid three invoices after this one that's still outstanding," she informed Becky.

"They're good customers, though," Becky said. "They'll pay eventually."

"Becky, I have a feeling they don't even know they owe you this money. Do you send them statements of account?"

Becky had not considered this possibility. "Well, no, I didn't want to bug them about it." She picked up the phone and called all of the customers who had accounts over 30 days.

form with carbon. If you are using a computer program, make certain that it prints at least two copies.

Accounting world

In accounting language, a financial transaction has occurred because you have traded something of value (the mug) for something of equivalent value (in this case, cash).

If you are a retailer and you use a cash register, you most likely will run a register report at the end of the day and record that day's transactions as a single item. If you are not using a cash register, you will record each sales transaction as it occurs.

The accounting entry generated for this type of sale is as follows:

DR	**Cash**	**$11.50**	
CR	**Sales**		**$10.00**
CR	**Sales tax liability**		**1.50**

This increases your sales total by the $10.00 that was the sales price of the item. The sales taxes that must be remitted to the government go into a liability account, because you have a liability to send them to the government later. (For more information on remittances, see Chapter 14.) The $11.50 is, of course, the amount of cash you received from the transaction. Notice that debits equal credits, maintaining the double-entry rule.

If you use a computerized system, there will most likely be a module called the sales journal. In this area, you will record the amount of the sale, the type and amount of taxes, and how the invoice was paid. This recording serves two functions. It provides the invoice to the customer as a record of the sale and it also records the accounting transaction at the same time. You just click a button to post the transaction to the accounting records and print off the invoice. All the debits and credits happen behind the scene but they still happen as described above.

Recording Credit Sales

This situation is not much different than cash sales.

Real life

A customer calls your warehouse and orders a case of 24 bottles of wine. You ship it out to the customer the next day FOB warehouse (see below for definition) with an invoice attached. Your invoice states that you have 30-day terms on your credit sales.

Accounting world

The criteria for a sale were met on the day the wine was shipped to the customer. You traded something of value (wine) for something of equal value (accounts receivable). Accounts receivable is an asset to you because it represents a promise to pay cash in the future.

A quick word about FOB: This term seems to be fading into the twilight, but the concept is important. FOB (free on board) indicates at what point the rights and responsibilities of ownership pass to the purchaser. For example, if something is shipped FOB warehouse, the vendor is declaring that the sale exists when the product leaves the warehouse. That is when the purchaser officially "bought" it. However, if it is shipped FOB destination, the vendor is declaring that he or she is responsible for the goods until they have been safely received at the purchaser's premises. In many purchase situations, this timing is not an issue, but you can see how it is important when goods are shipped overseas. Who is out of pocket if the ship sinks? If it was shipped FOB warehouse, then the purchaser is responsible for the loss (or, more likely, for purchasing insurance to cover the loss). If it was shipped FOB destination, the liability remains with the vendor.

In the example above, the goods were shipped FOB warehouse, so the transaction becomes a sale the day it is shipped. The accounting is as follows:

DR	**Accounts Receivable**	**$1,380.00**
CR	**Sales**	**$1,200.00**
CR	**Retail tax liability**	**180.00**

The details of the receivable would be listed in a sub-ledger, whether manual or computerized. The sub-ledger gives you a snapshot in time showing all amounts still receivable from customers and how old these receivables are (e.g., current, 30 days, 60 days, 90 days).

In a computer program, you will still go into the sales journal (just like the cash sale) and record the amount of the sale along with the type and amount of taxes, but you will not record a payment (because there hasn't been one yet). This will leave the amount showing as outstanding on the accounts receivable listing.

Sales Discounts

You can sometimes expedite your collections by offering your customers a discount for early payment. For example, if you offer 30-day terms, that means that your customers must pay your invoices in full within 30 days. However, you could offer terms such as 2/10 net 30, which means that your customers will get a 2 percent discount on their invoices if they pay you within 10 days; otherwise, the bill is due in full in 30 days.

Let's use the example from above. The customer's bill was $1,380, including retail taxes. The customer pays within 10 days and therefore takes the discount. You will know this because the customer sends you a check for $1,352.40 instead of one for $1,380. (Be aware, however, that frequently customers will try to stretch the discount, sending you a check after the 10 days is up.) You would have recorded the sale and account receivable in your books at the original invoice amount of $1,380. Remember that the original sales entry looked like this:

DR	**Accounts Receivable**	**$1,380.00**	
CR	**Sales**		**$1,200.00**
CR	**Retail tax liability**		**180.00**

But now you have a cash receipt of only $1,352.40. There are two ways to record this discount.

You know you need to take the full amount out of the receivable account because the customer doesn't owe you anymore. You could reverse the difference directly to the sales account (along with the associated retail sales tax). The entry would look like this:

DR	**Cash**	**$1,352.40**	
DR	**Sales**	**24.00**	
DR	**Retail tax liability**	**3.60**	
CR	**Accounts receivable**		**$1,380.00**

This reflects the reality of everything that has occurred.

The second (and preferred) method is to use a sales discount account for these types of transactions instead of the sales account. The sales discount account would be a contra account. It is a part of revenue but would serve to reduce revenue for the total amount of the discounts given in the period. All of the other pieces of the entry would remain the same. This method has the benefit of allowing you to see at a glance how much you have "given away" in discounts year-to-date rather than just mushing all your discounts in with sales.

Recording Cash Receipts

Once the money comes in from outstanding receivables, you must apply it to the accounting records to reduce the accounts receivable balance.

Real life

You open the mail when it is delivered and, lo and behold, there's a check from one of your customers for product they bought 30 days before. Let's say it's the same customer as in the above example. You fill out a deposit slip for the check and deposit it into the company's bank account.

Accounting world

Now you need to reflect the cash receipt in the books. The entry is as follows:

DR	**Cash**	**$1,380.00**	
CR	**Accounts receivable**		**$1,380.00**

You do not record anything in the sales account or the retail tax liability account because you have already done that in a prior period. You just need to reflect the increase in your bank account and the fact that the amount is no longer receivable.

In your sub-ledger, you will show that the amount was paid and the date of payment. If you are on a computerized system, you will go into the cash receipts journal and indicate the customer, date, amount of payment, and method of payment. The system will automatically record the entries to the journals and the accounts receivable sub-ledger.

Partial payments

A quick note regarding partial payments. There may be times when, for example, a customer owes you a total of $937.54 but will send you a check for $415.12. How do you apply this payment? If the customer has a good bookkeeping system, there will be invoice numbers written on the check so that you know to which invoices you should apply the payment. If not, you may need to do a quick scan of all the invoices outstanding for that customer. Starting with the oldest invoices, add up a few and see if you can recreate the amount of the check. If not, you will have to call the customer to find out which invoices he or she is trying to pay. This situation could mean that your customer's records differ from your own, and it might be a good opportunity to correct the problem.

However, if the customer owes you $937.54 and sends you a check for $500, you can assume that the customer is able to make only partial payment of his or her account. Apply the payment to the oldest invoices first.

Preparing Invoices

A quick word about the preparation of invoices. You should prepare the invoices as soon as possible after you have provided the service or product to the customer. One copy should be forwarded or presented to the customer, and one should be kept for your records. Your invoice will be more effective if you include as much detail as possible about the service or product provided, including dates of service (if applicable) or number of items. The invoice should also show any retail taxes separately.

Preparing Statements of Account

At the end of every month, it's important to know which customers still owe you money. You do this by looking at the aged accounts receivable report. This report will tell you who owes how much and how old the receivables are. If you are on a manual system, the aged accounts receivable report will simply be the sub-ledger that you prepared when you made your credit sales entries. If you're on a computerized system, this report will be one of your standard reports. Examine the receivables report at the end of the month. Are your receivables growing? Are they getting older? If so, why? If your terms are 30 days and you have many receivables aged 60 days or more, you may have some underlying collection problems that you must examine further.

Once you know who still owes you at the end of the month, it's important to make sure your customers remember, too. Prepare a statement of account for all customers who still owe you at the end of the month, not just for those who are overdue. Don't worry that your customers will think you are pushy. Sending a monthly statement of account is standard business practice, and your customers will expect it. In fact, if you don't do it, they might get the impression that you are disorganized.

The statement should show the dates of the original invoices and will indicate in which aging "bucket" the receivable belongs. Sample 10 shows a statement of account.

Use a highlighter to mark the amounts that are older than your credit terms allow. Many businesses have stickers printed up in bright colors with messages reminding the customer (gently) that the invoice is overdue. Having a strong statement of account system will make it much easier for you to get money in the door.

You need perform no accounting for these statements. They are simply reminders to customers of balances you have already recorded in your books. The only exception

Sample 10
STATEMENT OF ACCOUNT

Small Company Inc.
Statement of Account
30 November 2003

Herb & Mary Friedmann
2570 Chancery Lane
New York, NY 95050

Date	Invoice #	Original Amt	Payments	Outstanding
12 June 2003	1457	752.12	752.12	0.00
30 July 2003	1593	467.02	300.00	167.02
3 Nov 2003	1745	263.78	0.00	263.78
Totals		**$1,482.92**	**$1,052.12**	**$430.80**
	Current	**30 days**	**60 days**	**90 days**
$430.80	**$263.78**	**0.00**	**0.00**	**$167.02**

would be interest charges on overdue amounts. If it is your policy to charge customers interest on overdue accounts, you would book interest entries at the end of every month. The accounting would be as follows:

DR Accounts receivable

CR Interest income

You would also make sure the interest is appropriately applied to each customer's account in the sub-ledger.

Bad Debts: Analyzing Them and Writing Them off

It's a situation every small business owner dreads: A customer doesn't pay. But it happens.

I'm going to cross over into managing your business for a moment, because before I show you how to record bad debts in your books, I want to make sure that you have done everything you can to minimize them. There are some strategies that you should implement in your everyday management practices that will help.

Screen your customers

If you are selling large-ticket items or large-dollar services, do not grant automatic credit to everyone who comes in the door. It's a recipe for disaster. Screen your credit customers thoroughly. You can (with their permission) obtain a credit agency report showing any past credit problems. You can

CASE STUDY

Vivian waited patiently for Becky to get off the phone with the last of the overdue accounts.

"Well, how did you make out?" she asked.

"Wow! I should have done that a long time ago. Four of them forgot and will send checks tomorrow. One was holding back payment because he wasn't happy with the service. He assumed that we just didn't care because we never called about the payment. The last one has no money to pay us. It looks like his business is just about to fold. I'll have to let Joe know. I think the two of them were talking last week about doing more work. We would have lost that money too."

Vivian sat beside Becky at the computer. She showed her how to print off the accounts receivable report at the end of every month. She also showed her how to send statements of account to the delinquent clients every month. With the new software, it took only about ten minutes for the entire procedure. To make Becky feel better, Vivian taped a copy of the new accounts receivable report up on the wall.

also have them fill out an application and ask for supplier references. Make sure to call the references. Some businesses do not grant credit until the second or a later sale. Whatever you do, make sure you know enough about your new customers before you grant them credit.

Set credit limits

Giving your customers unlimited credit can leave your company vulnerable. It is far too easy for businesses operating in good faith to get in over their heads with credit. Some unscrupulous businesses search for suppliers with lax credit limits, then stockpile product. They run up a huge bill and never pay. You have little leverage at that point because they don't need anything else from you: you've already given it to them. Setting reasonable credit limits can help you avoid some of those problems.

Make your credit terms clear

Ensure that you have your terms on every invoice and statement that you produce. When you take on new customers, make sure you go over your policies with them. Sometimes, this simple step can help you avoid major misunderstandings.

Follow up with monthly statements

As described above, make sure that you send out monthly statements of account to your customers. Frequently, this simple reminder can produce results.

Call your customers when they are overdue

Don't be afraid to call your customers about overdue invoices. It ranks right up there with a root canal, but the old saying "the squeaky wheel gets the grease" applies here. Be consistent in your communication to your customers, and they will appreciate your businesslike attitude.

Get professional help

When all else fails, and you are pretty sure you have lost the customer anyway, turn the account over to a collection agency. Agencies will usually charge you a percentage of the amount they collect, but it is well worth it not to have to lose sleep over harassing the customer for money.

Pursue the debt in small claims court

Every jurisdiction has different rules for which matters can be brought to small claims court and what the procedures are for doing so. If you feel that you have a strong case and the customer has money to pay the bill (there's no point trying to get blood out of a stone), you may wish to pursue this option. If the judge rules for you, the customer will have a judgment against him or her ordering payment to be made to you. If the customer still doesn't pay, he or she will face repercussions from the court.

Writing off the debt

If you finally get to the point where you think there is no hope (either the customer has skipped the country or gone bankrupt), it is time for you to write off the account.

The accounting entry is as follows:

DR Bad debt expense

DR Sales tax liability

CR Accounts receivable

This action removes the invoices from the accounts receivable balance and records the expense on the income statement. You must do this because the income was recorded in the income statement when the sale was made. When it becomes uncollectible, the net income should be reduced accordingly. The entry also removes the amount that you have posted as owing to the government for sales taxes. You won't get the money now, so you certainly do not need to give it to the government.

Chapter Summary

- The sales cycle is the portion of the operating cycle that turns product into receivables into cash.
- For accounting purposes, a sale is recognized when the risks and rewards of ownership of the goods changes hands.
- Partial payments from customers should be applied to the oldest invoices first.
- The accounts receivable sub-ledger should be reviewed regularly and delinquent accounts followed up on promptly and consistently.

Chapter 9

Recording the Purchases Cycle

In this chapter, you will learn —

- The components of the purchases cycle
- How to account for cash and credit purchases
- How to track accounts payable

Take another look at Figure 1 in Chapter 8 to refresh your memory of the operating cycle. Just as the sales cycle forms one half, the purchases cycle forms the other half.

The purchases cycle encompasses many activities in the business:

- Purchasing inventory and supplies
- Recording the purchase entries
- Paying accounts payable
- Tracking cash payment

This chapter looks at each of these activities and their associated bookkeeping in turn.

Purchasing Inventory

One of the most important functions of a retail or manufacturing business is the purchase of inventory. Without inventory, there are no sales.

To understand inventory, you must also look at cost of goods sold. These two are like the ends of a teeter-totter. In theory, when goods are purchased for manufacture or resale, they go into inventory. When they are sold, they are taken out of inventory and plunked into cost of goods sold (COGS). Therefore, at the end of every period, the balance in the inventory account represents the cost of the items left in inventory. The amount in cost of goods sold represents the cost of those items that appear in the revenue line. (For an in-depth look at valuation of inventory, see Chapter 10.)

CASE STUDY

Vivian wasn't going to let Becky get away with her current accounts payable system either. Becky kept all of the current payables in a red file folder that sat on her desk. She tried to keep the pile sorted by date, placing the ones that needed payment sooner on the top, but she didn't always get around to organizing it properly. Last month, she had even paid her sales tax remittance late, and got hit with a 10 percent penalty, plus interest.

Once paid, the invoices went into files sorted by vendor name in the filing cabinet. The miscellaneous file was the fullest. There were many vendors that Joe and Becky had purchased from only once, and those invoices all ended up in that file.

Vivian had Becky pull out all the files to look through them. She asked Becky how much she had paid so far in the year in late fees and penalties because she had paid invoices late. Becky shook her head. She had no idea.

There are two main systems for managing the accounting of inventory: the perpetual inventory system and the periodic inventory system. The larger the company, the more likely it is to use the perpetual inventory system.

The perpetual inventory system adjusts the inventory every time an inventory transaction occurs. Doing so allows the inventory and COGS accounts to be accurate at any point in time.

When inventory is purchased, the entry to account for the purchase is as follows:

DR	**Inventory**	**$4,750.00**	
DR	**Retail sales taxes recoverable**	**332.50**	
CR	**Cash (or Accounts payable)**		**$5,082.50**

Obviously, you would credit the bank account if you purchased the inventory with cash and the accounts payable account if you purchased it on credit.

When inventory is sold, the entry would be as follows:

DR	**COGS**	**$4,750.00**	
CR	**Inventory**		**$4,750.00**

This action places the sold goods onto the income statement where those costs belong.

A periodic inventory system is easier to account for and manage. All inventory purchases are posted to the COGS account until the end of the year, when the inventory is counted and an adjustment is made. The entry for the purchase of inventory would then be as follows:

DR	**COGS**	**$4,750.00**	
DR	**Retail sales taxes recoverable**	**332.50**	
CR	**Cash (or Accounts payable)**		**$5,082.50**

At the end of the period (usually the year, but sometimes the month), the actual inventory on hand is counted and the cost calculated. The adjustment to actual is then made through the COGS account, which then makes both accounts correct. For example, if actual inventory on hand at the end of the year was $52,450, and your books reflected the inventory total from last year of $41,231, the entry to correct both the inventory and the cost of goods sold account would be as follows:

DR	**Inventory**	**$11,219.00**	
CR	**COGS**		**$11,219.00**

The fact that you need to do this adjustment tells you that you didn't sell as much as you purchased in the year. Some of the goods were still in inventory at the end of the year. Your entry corrects this difference.

Purchasing Supplies

There are hundreds of other purchases that a small-business owner needs to make in a year other than inventory purchases. These include office supplies, rent, utilities, and office cleaning services. Recording these items is straightforward:

DR	**Office supplies (or whichever category)**	**$12.95**
DR	**Retail sales taxes recoverable**	**0.91**
CR	**Cash (or Accounts payable)**	**$13.86**

If you work with a computerized system, you will not only be able to summarize purchases by account category, you will also have the ability to summarize by vendor. This is good information to have. It lets you compare the volume of purchases by each vendor.

Common Cost of Goods Sold Categories

Cost of goods sold (COGS) is usually compressed to a single line on the income statement, but it might have several components to it. If you are a retailer or wholesaler, your only COGS would be your purchases. If you are a service business, you will have no COGS. However, if you are a manufacturer, you will have several categories of expenses directly related to the manufacture of the products sold. Here are the most common ones:

Purchases: Purchases represents the cost of the goods purchased for resale or the raw materials purchased for manufacturing, but only for those goods that were sold during the year. Costs for goods still on the premises remain in the inventory account until those goods are sold.

Direct labor: This category is the wage and benefit cost of your employees related to the manufacture of the goods your company makes. Again, the labor costs of those goods still on the premises are in the inventory account. If you have one employee that makes all your goods, and that employee worked on the goods sold as well as the goods in inventory, how can you apportion the employee's salary to each category? Most manufacturers set up a "standard cost" so that they can split the labor costs between sold items and inventoried items. Determining a standard cost requires some analysis of total units produced versus total wage costs. You must come up with a labor cost per unit. You know how many units are still in inventory (because you've counted them), so you apply that cost accordingly. A more detailed discussion of standard costing is beyond the scope of this book.

Other manufacturing costs: Large manufacturers tend to apportion as many expenses as possible between operating costs and cost of goods sold. For example, the electricity cost related to the plant could be viewed as a direct cost of manufacture, whereas the electricity cost of the front office is not. This discussion involves management accounting concepts more than bookkeeping concepts, and as such, is outside the scope of this book.

Common Expense Categories

Although you can call your expense groupings anything you want, it makes sense to use some of the standard categories. When it comes time to prepare the tax return, you will have to fit your expenses into these categories anyway.

Here are some of the common expense groupings:

Advertising and promotion: Includes expenses for newspaper ads, telephone directory ads, raffle prizes, and anything else done for publicity. Some businesses also include expenses for their business cards and letterhead here.

Amortization and depreciation: Includes expense for the current year for both capital assets and other assets (such as incorporation costs).

Bad debts: See Chapter 8 for a discussion of bad debts.

Business taxes, fees, licenses: Includes expenses for any licenses you may require to do business in your municipality and any special commercial taxes.

Equipment repairs: Includes expenses for any work that needs to be done on the shop machinery or computer and office equipment.

Home office expenses: This category is discussed in more depth in Chapter 13.

Interest expense: Includes interest charged on overdrafts, bank loans, or mortgages on property in which the company operates.

Meals and entertainment: Includes expenses for those events to which you take customers (or potential customers) or suppliers. These expenses must be separated out from other expenses because in most jurisdictions, this category receives special tax treatment.

Office services: Includes fees paid to any person or company you hire to provide services for the office, such as bookkeeping and other contract work.

Office supplies: Includes pens, paper, note pads, coffee, and other small supplies.

Professional fees: Includes accounting and legal fees. If you pay for outside bookkeeping services, that expense falls into office services.

Property taxes: Includes tax costs if you own the building in which your business operates.

Repairs and maintenance: Includes all repairs except equipment repairs. Examples would be painting offices, landscape supplies, and refinishing a desk.

CASE STUDY

Vivian and Becky looked through all of the vendor invoices and statements for the year. Vivian calculated that so far that year, Joe and Becky had paid more than $2,000 in interest and penalties to vendors for late payments. There had been a few times that they had to pay late because of cash flow crunches, but most of the interest was charged because the invoice had been lost or forgotten.

Becky had felt terrible about having cost the business so much money by not having a good tracking system. Vivian told her not to worry any more. They would set up a new system together that would almost automatically track payables.

Later that afternoon, Becky printed off her new accounts payable listing from *QuickBooks*. She couldn't believe that all the information about what they owed to their vendors was now on a single piece of paper. The list was sorted by vendor and also showed how old the payables were, so she could tell if she and Joe were getting behind.

Even better was that she could enter each vendor's credit terms so that *QuickBooks* would proactively warn her that an invoice would soon be due. No more late fees!

Rent: If you are renting your business premises.

Shop supplies (manufacturers only): Includes the dozens of small items that you must buy for the plant that are not directly related to the items you manufacture (e.g., oil for the machinery, paper towels, staples for an electric stapler, etc.).

Telephone expense: This category is self-explanatory, but you would most likely include all telephone-related expenses here: phone lines, fax lines, cell phone charges, Internet charges, pager charges. Remember that if the charge for your phone book ad appears on your phone bill, you should separate it out into the advertising and promotion category.

Travel: Includes hotel, car rental, and other costs of business trips. The meals expense would go into the meals and entertainment category.

Utilities: Includes electricity, heat, or water in your business premises, if you are required to pay for these things.

Vehicle expenses: Includes, if your company owns the vehicle, fuel, vehicle repairs and maintenance, license fee, lease costs or the interest on any financing loan, insurance, and other costs to maintain the vehicle. (If you personally own the vehicle and are using it partly for business purposes, it requires special treatment. See Chapter 13 for more details.)

Wages and benefits: Includes the costs of maintaining your employees: gross wages, employer health tax, worker's compensation premiums, payroll taxes, and any other cost related to your employees. If you have subcontract labor, that cost should go into cost of goods sold (if it's directly related to the manufacturing

Sample 11
ACCOUNTS PAYABLE REPORT

Small Company Inc.
Accounts Payable Report
31 December 2003

Vendor	Current	30 days	60 days	90 days	Total
ABC Corp.	517.12		125.75		642.87
City Electrical	2,257.10				2,257.10
Festival Marketing		212.96			212.96
Good Ads Inc.	4,957.23				4,957.23
Jones Goodhouse				2,712.56	2,712.56
Networks Plus	1,019.75				1,019.75
Phonenet	124.75	124.75	124.75		374.25
Supply World	3,610.23				3,610.23
TTE Manufacturing	5,284.25				5,284.25
Totals	**$17,770.43**	**$337.71**	**$250.50**	**$2,712.56**	**$21,071.20**

process) or office expenses (if it's office-related labor). This split will make it easier for you to reconcile this account to your payroll records at the end of the year.

Setting up the Accounts Payable Sub-ledger

The accounts payable sub-ledger will look much like the accounts receivable sub-ledger. If you're on a manual system, you will create a listing of outstanding accounts that you need to pay and will include information on how old they are (their age). If you're on a computerized system, this is one of your standard reports. Sample 11 shows an accounts payable report.

Notice that the report has the same aging "buckets" as the receivables report (discussed in Chapter 8). It's as important to know how old your payables are as it is to know how old your receivables are. If your creditors are extending 30-day terms and most of your payables are more than 90 days old, you may have a cash flow problem that needs further investigation.

Cash Payments

Paying your accounts payable is a relatively easy task. Once again, here are real life and accounting world examples.

Real life

You write a check to your supplier and mail it off. You mark on the invoice the date paid, the check number, and the amount paid.

Accounting world

The entry to remove the amount from the payables is —

DR	**Accounts payable**	**$1,435.12**	
CR	**Cash**		**$1,435.12**

You would also update your accounts payable sub-ledger to show that you had paid the amount. If you are on a manual system, the accounts payable sub-ledger will simply be the list that you created when you set up the payables. If you are on a computerized system, it will be one of your standard reports.

A computerized system provides a few extra benefits here. First, if you have set up a laser printer and have purchased laser-print checks, you can print off the check from your accounting system. It will record the payment in the books at the same time, saving you a few extra steps. You will also be able to look at how much you spend per month, per vendor, or per category more easily than with a manual system.

Chapter Summary

- ➡ If you sell products, inventory and cost of goods sold are important categories to track in your accounting system.
- ➡ Cost of goods sold can be broken into subcategories: purchases, direct labor, and other manufacturing costs.
- ➡ Purchases should be separated by category in the bookkeeping system.
- ➡ It's important to continually review your accounts payable listing to ensure you are not incurring unnecessary interest and penalties on late payments.

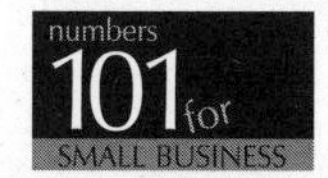

Chapter 10

Inventory

In this chapter, you will learn —

- The two main accounting systems for tracking inventory
- At what cost to report your inventory
- How to value your inventory at the end of the period
- How to set up and calculate a physical count at the end of the period

If you sell goods, the management of your inventory is crucial to your business's success. This chapter examines in-depth the methods of inventory tracking, valuation, and counting.

Inventory is a concept as well as a physical pile of goods. Many unscrupulous companies manipulate their inventory figures for the purpose of changing values on their financial statements. Understanding the underlying concept will help you not only to operate your business more efficiently, but also to read other companies' financials with new eyes.

Inventory Tracking Systems

The previous chapter touched on inventory tracking systems because they relate to how cost of goods sold is recorded.

This chapter will look at them in more detail. If your company deals with goods, you will have to choose your method for calculating how much inventory you have on hand.

Types of Inventory

Inventory means different things to different industries:

- If you are a retailer or wholesaler, you buy goods and re-sell them. Your inventory cost represents the goods you have bought for resale but have not yet sold.
- If you are a service business, most likely inventory will not be a consideration. However, some service

CASE STUDY

Becky was confused. Vivian had asked her to do an inventory count to input into *QuickBooks*. Becky looked around the workshop at the boxes of washers, pipefittings, and insulating covers. She had no idea where to start. Some of this stuff had been around for four years. The box of washers on top of the stack would have been bought sometime this year, but the one on the bottom was old. The prices paid for the two boxes would have been significantly different.

Becky opened a bin in the corner. In it was a tangled pile of pipe ends, sawed off in the installation process. What could they possibly be worth?

She would need to call Vivian to get some more help with the process. As she picked up the phone, she looked at the bag full of office supplies she had just purchased at the supply store. Was that inventory too? She dialed the phone.

industries, such as the legal and accounting industries, track the time that has been spent on client work but not yet billed as inventory.

- If you are a manufacturer, you will most likely have several categories of inventory (see the next section).

Inventory in a Manufacturing Environment

If you make goods and sell them, you will have goods in different stages of completion at any particular time. There are three main categories of inventory for a manufacturer:

- **Raw materials inventory:** This category will include raw materials you have purchased but which are still sitting on the shop floor. For example, if you make furniture, you will still have lumber that you have purchased before the end of the year that you have not started to work on.
- **Goods-in-process:** At the end of the year, you will also have goods that you have started to produce, but have not yet completed. Going back to our furniture manufacturer, she may have 24 dining room tables for which the tops and pedestals have been completed but have not yet been attached to each other. These are goods-in-process. Goods-in-process may have a labor and overhead component to them as well as some work and expense already invested in them.
- **Finished goods inventory:** These are exactly what the term says they are: finished goods. These are items that were completed and ready for sale but which had not been sold at the end of the period.

Now that you know what's in your inventory, how do you track it? There are two main methods:

- **Periodic inventory method:** This method is the simplest. When you purchase goods or raw materials, you put them into the COGS (cost of goods sold) account. At the end of the period, you take a physical inventory count and make an adjustment between the inventory account and

COGS to correct both accounts to actual. The benefit of this method is its simplicity. The downside is that the balance sheet and income statement will be correct only at the end of the period. At any point during the year, the COGS could be misleading, perhaps indicating that the expense is higher than it actually is.

- **Perpetual inventory method:** This method requires more accounting transactions and is more difficult for small businesses. Under this method, when you purchase goods or materials, you make an accounting entry to increase the inventory account. When you make a sale, you make an entry to remove the cost of the item from inventory and put it into COGS. In theory, both inventory and cost of goods sold should be correct at any particular moment. At the end of the year, you take a physical inventory count to compare against the two accounts. You would adjust any difference to actual in the books at the end of the year.

Advances in technology are making perpetual systems easier to use. Many bar code systems now link to the accounting records and automatically deduct the item from inventory when it is sold.

Which system is right for your business? You must weigh the benefit of having more timely and accurate information against the cost and aggravation of tracking that information. If you have a bar code system, the perpetual system will work well for you. It will also work well if you sell big-ticket, slow-moving items, due to the small volume of extra transactions involved. However, if you sell many small items and are bookkeeping manually, the periodic system will suit your needs and won't make you crazy!

Inventory Costing Methods

At first blush, it may seem silly to have to discuss how inventory is costed. It is clearly valued at the actual cost of purchase, including shipping and freight, duty, and insurance. However, a problem arises when many of the same goods are purchased throughout the year at different prices. Which of those are considered to be the ones sold during the year?

Let's say you made purchases of Product A throughout the year as follows:

- 500 units on January 15 at $12.50/unit (total: $6,250)
- 1,250 units on April 10 for $13.10/unit (total: $16,375)
- 375 units on July 29 for $12.16/unit (total: $4,560)
- 950 units on November 12 for $14.25/unit (total: $13,537.50)

You know, therefore, that you've increased your inventory over the year by 3,075 units for a total cost of $40,722.50 ($6,250 + $16,375 + $4,560 + $13,537.50).

Let's assume that this is your first year in business and you started with no inventory. Let's also assume that you sold 2,010 of your 3,075 units during the year. Your ending inventory then is clearly 1,065 units (3,075 – 2,010). But what cost do you assign to these 1,065 units?

There are four major methods used to cost inventory flows: specific-identification; first-in, first-out; last-in, first-out; and weighted average cost. Each method has rules about when it should be applied.

Specific identification method

This method is theoretically the most correct of all. It tracks each individual item in inventory, and when that particular item is sold, that is the item that is taken out of inventory. If you know that your 1,065 units are made up of 210 of the $12.50 units, 345 of the $13.10 units, 312 of the $12.16 units, and 198 of the $14.25 units, then your inventory is the sum of all of these: $13,759.92.

Specific identification is universally permissible, but can be difficult or impossible when there are large quantities of items to track.

First-in, first-out (FIFO)

This method allows you to assume that the first items put into inventory are the first ones out the door. Using the example above, you know you have sold 2,010 units. This means that you have sold all 500 of the $12.50 units, all 1,250 of the $13.10 units, and 260 of the $12.16 units. That leaves you with inventory of 115 of the $12.16 units and all 950 of the $14.25 units. Your total inventory value is therefore $14,935.90.

FIFO is the costing method used by most businesses. It makes sense when you think about it, as you will most likely rotate your stock; that is, you will sell your oldest stock first to keep your products in good condition.

In times of changing prices, FIFO gives you the inventory valuation most resembling replacement value, because the inventory items are costed at the most recent costs.

Last-in, first-out (LIFO)

This method is the opposite of FIFO. It assumes that your most recent purchases are the first ones you sold. Under the LIFO method, you would have sold all 950 of the $14.25 units, all 375 of the $12.16 units, and 685 of the $13.10 units. This leaves you with an inventory of 565 of the $13.10 units and all 500 of the $12.50 units, giving you a total inventory cost of $13,651.50.

LIFO is the method that provides you with the most accurate picture of your gross margin because the items at the most recent cost are the ones applied to the revenues. However, it can leave an extremely distorted picture of the inventory value. If you always have rising inventory levels, you may end up with inventory valued on the balance sheet at prices that are 10 or 20 years old. These values never "clear out" of the inventory. If, for some reason, sales are higher than current production, you will "dip" into that old layer, and the COGS on the income statement will bear extremely little resemblance to reality.

LIFO is quite a popular method of costing in the United States, but in Canada is disallowed for taxation purposes, and therefore is not used in Canada.

Weighted average cost

This method tries to correct the inequities of FIFO and LIFO and comes up with an average cost for the year. Then, as units are sold, that average cost is applied to the income statement. In the example above, you have a total of 3,075 units that you have brought into inventory. The total cost of those units is $40,722.50. The average cost is then $40,722.50/3,075 = $13.24 per unit. You sold 2,010 units in the year, so your cost of goods sold would be $13.24 X 2,010 = $26,612.40 which would leave $14,110.10 ($40,722.50 – $26,612.40) in inventory.

CASE STUDY

Becky dusted herself off after taking the bin of pipe ends to the curb to be taken to the dump. After checking with Vivian, she realized these pieces were useless and had no accounting value. One less thing to have to count.

Vivian had helped Becky set up a count sheet for her inventory. On it was listed each type of part that Joe usually stocked. Vivian told her to ignore any office supplies and shop supplies and count only the parts. That would certainly make the job easier!

They had discussed how the inventory should be costed. They settled on the average cost method, for two reasons. First, the inventory was small and of low dollar value. It wasn't necessary to keep either the balance sheet or the income statement at replacement value. Second, the average cost method made the count easier. It would not be necessary for Becky to segregate each purchase of small parts from the others. She would just find the average per-unit price of each part and would cost the inventory at that value.

Becky turned up the radio and started her count.

Confused yet? Inventory costing can be a very confusing topic. The good thing is that it is becoming less of an issue in the business world, in part because ease of shipping allows inventory to be shipped in a very short amount of time, so you no longer need to stockpile great loads of product. During the last 20 years, in most industries in most industrialized countries, inventory levels have been diminishing.

Just know that once you pick a costing method, you'll have clear sailing from there and never have to think about the alternative methods again!

Year-End Valuation

We won't spend much time on this issue, but it's important to know that accounting rules in most countries require you to review your inventory valuation at the end of the year and compare its cost to its current market value. If the market value (the value you expect to sell it for) is less than its cost, you are required to write down your inventory to that value. This valuation is called the lower of cost or market (LCM).

You may have inventory that's worth less than you paid for it for a number of reasons. You may still be carrying older models of some items when new models are now available. This might be the case if you sell computers or cars. Your inventory might have been damaged somehow, and you will have to sell it for less. A bookstore might have this problem.

The purpose of this rule is to make sure that companies are not inflating their balance sheets with inventory that is not worth at least the cost on the balance sheet.

Setting up the Inventory Count

Regardless of which costing or tracking method you use for your inventory, you must perform a physical count at the end of the year. Accounting rules require you to do this, but it also makes sense from a management perspective. You want to make certain that you do not have employees walking away with inventory. You also want to make sure that if you have a perpetual inventory tracking system, it's working. If you come

Sample 12
INVENTORY COUNT SHEET

Small Company Inc.
Inventory Count Sheet
31 December 2003

Carried forward: ______________

Part #	Description	Unit count	Price per unit	Total
129A	Server sensors	412	0.14	57.68
475J1	Banders	6	27.95	167.70
973B	Gorlon Flexers	18	12.99	233.82
429F	Merton Caps	97	56.10	5,441.70
429A	Coag Drills	28	19.25	539.00
712C	Dorsters (large)	0	312.47	0.00
19B	Dorsters (small)	219	1.75	383.25
25A1	Finger Mites	37	42.10	1,557.70
965G2	Prop Guides	129	0.73	94.17
Total				**8,475.02**

up with radically different counts than your system calculates, you know you have an underlying problem that you must solve.

When preparing for your inventory count, you should understand the concept of cut off. You want to make sure that you are counting only the items that are actually in inventory at the end of the year. If you are performing your count the day before or the day after year end, you will need to thoroughly track the sales of those days so that you do not count items that have been sold or miss counting items that are there. To avoid this problem, many retailers shut down for their inventory counts. If your business has a December 31st year-end, you will not face this problem, because the next day is generally a holiday. The entire day can be used to count the inventory.

The first step in the process is to prepare the count sheets. On these sheets should be a listing of all types of inventory items. If you are on a perpetual inventory system, you would include a column for the number of units you expect to have. You will leave a blank column for the count itself, followed by a column with the per-unit costs as determined by the costing method you are using. The final column is called the extension column. You will extend the count times the per-unit cost into this column. Sample 12 shows a typical count sheet.

Notice that there is space at the bottom of the page to total up all of the items on that page. The cumulative count from any previous pages should be shown at the top of each page. You will add this figure to the total on the bottom of the page, then carry the sum of these two to the next page.

If you are using a spreadsheet program like Microsoft Excel, the extensions and totals will calculate by formula automatically. If you would like an Excel template to download, please go to my website at www.numbers101.com and click on "Cool Biz Tools."

If you use a manual system, make use of Worksheet 1, a blank inventory count sheet. Photocopy as many as you require to complete your count.

It's always a good idea to have a second person check both your counts and your math, especially when you are dealing with significant amounts of inventory. It's quite easy to make a mistake. If your financial statements are being audited by an outside accounting firm, a representative from the firm will most likely observe the count and perform some test counts on behalf of the firm. It's not that the firm doesn't trust you; it simply has the job of making sure the count is done correctly.

Now that you have an inventory total, you will make your inventory figures in your books equal that total. If you're on a periodic system, you will always have to do this adjustment at the end of the period. If you're on a perpetual system, the count should be the same as the calculated amount, and no adjustment will be necessary. If it is different, you will still need to adjust to the actual count, then review your tracking system to find out why there are differences.

Chapter Summary

- There are two main systems for tracking your inventory: the perpetual inventory method and the periodic inventory method.
- There are several ways to cost your inventory. Every tax jurisdiction will have rules as to which methods are acceptable for income tax purposes.
- In many countries, inventory must be valued at the lower of cost or market value in order to follow GAAP.
- The inventory must be counted at the end of the year and the books must reflect the actual count.

Worksheet 1
INVENTORY COUNT SHEET

Company Name:
Inventory Count Sheet
Date:

		A	B	A X B
Part #	**Description**	**Unit Count**	**Price/unit**	**Total**
Total this page				
Carried forward from previous page				
Total Inventory (carry forward to next page)				

Chapter 11

Capital Assets

In this chapter, you will learn —

- What capital assets are
- How to set up capital assets on your balance sheet
- What's included in the cost of a capital asset
- Methods of depreciation
- How to account for the sale of an asset

Most businesses have capital assets (also known by older names: fixed assets or property, plant, and equipment). Capital assets are tangible assets (i.e., you can see them and feel them) that have value to the business for more than the current year.

Capital assets include the following:

- Land
- Buildings
- Machinery
- Furniture
- Vehicles
- Computer equipment
- Computer software
- Leasehold improvements

These are all capital assets because they all have use to the business in future years as well as in the current year (unlike, for example, pens and paper, which you will use up quickly).

What complicates the accounting for capital assets is the concept of depreciation, a recognition that these assets will eventually wear out. Depreciation is discussed later in this chapter.

What's in the Cost of My Capital Assets?

The simple answer is that the cost of a capital asset is the outlay of cash (or accounts payable) you must make for the asset. For example, if you go to the office supply store

CASE STUDY

Becky looked at her list of capital assets. Vivian had asked her to make the list, using prior years' tax returns and the old files. Becky had been able to find the original cost of all the capital assets and calculated how much depreciation had already been taken.

The only problem she was having was with an asset they had purchased this year: a generator for the workshop. It was a huge monster and took up the entire corner of the little room. Becky remembered that Vivian had said something about including all of the "satellite costs" in the asset cost. Joe had to bring in an electrician to hard wire the generator. They also had to drill a hole to the outside and attach plastic tubing so that the generator could vent itself.

Even if Becky could figure that out, she still had to decide which method and rate to use to depreciate the generator. She would ask Vivian when the accountant came back later in the afternoon.

and buy a new desk for $100 (ignore taxes for now), the entry in the general journal would be —

DR	**Furniture & fixtures**	**$100.00**	
CR	**Cash**		**$100.00**

Satellite costs

There may also be other costs involved in buying an asset and getting it ready for use. For example, when you buy a piece of specialized machinery, there might be shipping costs as well as the cost of an electrician to install it and get it working. These "satellite" costs would also be included in the cost of the asset. They are considered fundamental to the purchase of the asset and not a period cost.

Satellite costs also commonly occur with the purchase of land and buildings. There are many extra costs that could be part of the purchase, such as legal fees, realtor fees, appraisal costs, zoning charges, and building permits. These are all considered to be a part of the sale, and you would include them in the cost of the asset. Setting up the purchase entry for a land and building purchase might look like this:

DR	**Land**	**$27,500.00**	
DR	**Building (cost)**	**93,450.00**	
DR	**Building (satellites)**	**4,923.00**	
CR	**Cash (downpayment)**		**$30,000.00**
CR	**Mortgage payable**		**95,873.00**

Trade-ins

Determining the cost of a capital asset gets a little more complicated when trade-ins are taken into account. A typical example is the purchase of a vehicle. You might trade in your old vehicle and pay (or finance) the difference. Accounting rules state that the value of assets purchased is equal to the value of the assets given up. For example, if your old truck is on the books at $4,000, and you trade it and a check for $10,000 for a new vehicle, the new vehicle gets set up on the books at $14,000, regardless of the list price of the new truck. Because there is already $4,000 in the vehicle account (related to the old truck), you would make the following entry to account for the cash component:

DR	**Vehicle**	**$10,000.00**	
CR	**Cash**		**$10,000.00**

Depreciation: An Overview

All assets, except for land, eventually wear out. Even your warehouse, which may stand for more than a hundred years, will one day fall under the wrecker's ball because it is too old and decrepit to be of use to your business.

Depreciation is the process of allocating the cost of the asset slowly into expense over the useful life of that asset. It makes intuitive sense that you should be allowed an expense for the decline in usefulness of an asset as it ages. However, it's important not to confuse the concept of depreciation with market value. Market value has no bearing on the financial statements, which in most cases report historical cost.

To facilitate the depreciation of assets, you need to group them according to their expected useful lives. A building has a much longer useful life than a computer has. Each grouping of capital assets will have its own depreciation method and rate. The common groupings are as follows:

Land

This grouping is self-explanatory. It is the land owned by the company that is used in the production of income. Land under the warehouse and plant would be included, but land bought in cottage country for speculation would not. Land always goes into a category by itself because it is the only asset that does not decline in value over time and thus is not depreciated.

Buildings

This grouping includes all buildings belonging to the company, but not the land they sit on (see above). All major renovations and improvements to the buildings over the years would be included in this account as well.

Equipment

All of the machinery and other productive equipment go into this grouping. Office equipment has its own category.

Tools

Generally, tools that cost more than $200 go in this category. Anything under that limit gets expensed on the income statement as small tools.

Office equipment

Fax machines, photocopiers, binding machines, and the like belong here. Computer equipment is placed in a separate category.

Signage

All signs made for the business (again, costing more than $200) should be capitalized into this account because the signs have a useful life extending over several years. The majority of small-business bookkeepers mistakenly expense these costs into advertising and promotion.

Computer hardware

This category encompasses all computer components except for software. It includes monitors, hard drives, CPUs, mouses (or mice, depending on your preference), and keyboards.

Computer software

This category includes the programs that you buy for your computer: accounting, CAD, spreadsheet, and email programs. Computer software is in a separate category from hardware because it is generally recognized that it becomes obsolete faster than hardware.

Vehicles

This includes trucks, trailers, passenger vehicles, ATVs, and other motorized vehicles that the company owns.

Now that you know how to categorize your capital assets, you need to look at the concepts involved in depreciation as well as the various methods of depreciation. Don't worry: It's not hard. Grab another coffee, and let's go!

Concepts Involved in Depreciation

There are a couple of concepts that you need to tackle before looking at depreciation methods. These are the concepts of useful life and salvage value.

Useful life

Useful life is an estimation of how long an asset will be used by the company before it is useless and must be thrown away or sold. For tax purposes, each category (or class) of asset has its own estimation of useful life. The useful life of a building is much greater than the useful life of a computer software program. For accounting purposes, it is generally easier to use the same basis of depreciation as the tax authorities use; otherwise, you will be reconciling the two every year end. Check with your accountant on the tax rules in your country.

Salvage value

Salvage value is established when the asset is purchased. It is an estimate of the value (if any) of the asset at the end of its useful life with the company. For example, a truck may be useful to the company for five years, at which point the owner expects to sell it for $7,500. That would be its salvage value.

Methods of Depreciation

There are three main methods of depreciating capital assets: straight-line, declining balance, and sum-of-the-years-digits. These methods are more prevalent than others because they are acceptable to most tax authorities.

Straight-line

This method is the simplest of the three. It takes the original cost of the asset less its expected salvage value (see above for the definition) and divides it by the number of years in its expected useful life. In the above example of the truck, if you purchased it for $27,000, the depreciable value would be $27,000 – $7,500, or $19,500. This amount would be divided by the useful life of five years to come to an annual depreciation amount of $3,900. Every year, you would take a $3,900 expense on your income statement to reflect the depreciation on the truck.

Declining balance

This method, as well as the sum-of-the-years-digits, is called an accelerated depreciation method because, by nature of its calculation, it allows more depreciation in earlier years and less in later years.

The declining balance method (sometimes called the double declining balance method, but meaning the same thing) applies a constant percentage to the declining book value of the asset.

Let's go back to the truck example above. If your depreciation rate is 20 percent, the depreciation over the five years that you own the truck would look like this:

Year	Percentage	Book value	Depreciation
1	20%	$27,000	$5,400
2	20%	21,600	4,320
3	20%	17,280	3,456
4	20%	13,824	2,765
5	20%	11,059	2,212

The book value at the end of the five years is $8,847. If you sell the vehicle for $7,500 at the end of the five years, you have a loss on sale because the book value is higher than the sale price. Remember that book value has no relationship to market value. If you sold the vehicle for $9,500, you would have taken too much depreciation over the years and would have a gain on sale. This is one area where tax treatment among countries differs significantly, so you should discuss this issue with your accountant. This chapter addresses only the general concepts of depreciation.

Sum-of-the-years-digits (SYD)

This method is used less frequently than it once was. It applies a declining portion of the total cost of the asset less the salvage value to depreciation expense.

In the example above, there are five years to depreciate. The sum of the years is 15 (1 + 2 + 3 + 4 + 5 = 15). A factor is used for each year starting with the highest number. In the example, depreciation over the five years would look like this:

Year	Factor	Cost minus salvage	Depreciation Expense
1	5/15	$19,500	$6,500
2	4/15	19,500	5,200
3	3/15	19,500	3,900
4	2/15	19,500	2,600
5	1/15	19,500	1,300

Notice that in both the straight-line and SYD methods, the total depreciation at the end of the five years equals the cost minus the salvage value. In the straight-line method, the total or accumulated depreciation is $3,900 X 5 = $19,500. In the SYD method, accumulated depreciation is $6,500 + 5,200 + 3,900 + 2,600 + 1,300 = $19,500. In the declining balance method, you ultimately get to the same place if you actually sell the vehicle for its estimated salvage value. Your accumulated depreciation is $5,400 + 4,320 + 3,456 + 2,765 + 2,212 = $18,153, which is less total depreciation than under the other two methods. However, if you sell the truck for $7,500, you will recognize a loss on sale of $1,347, which, when added to your accumulated depreciation, will give you $19,500.

All depreciation methods end up getting the book value of the asset down to its salvage value. They all just take different roads to get there.

Accounting for Depreciation

Now that you know how you are depreciating your capital assets, it's time to look at the accounting that you need to do.

On the balance sheet, there are contra accounts for each group of assets. You will remember that a contra account nets off the balance of another account. It is in these contra accounts that you accumulate the depreciation on each grouping of assets. For example, you might see on your balance sheet:

Capital assets

Equipment	$12,575
Accumulated depreciation: equipment	(8,715)
Computer hardware	6,412
Accumulated depreciation: CH	(1,972)
Vehicle	27,000
Accumulated depreciation: vehicle	(3,900)
Total capital assets	**$31,400**

Keeping the accumulated depreciation separated into an account of its own allows you to see the original cost of that pool of assets as well as the total amount that has been depreciated to date. If you were to read another company's financial statements, this separation would give you a little more information as to the size of the asset base and the age of the assets.

When the depreciation has been calculated for the year, the entry in the general journal to record it is —

DR Depreciation expense

CR Accumulated depreciation (A/D)

You would credit the accumulated depreciation accounts appropriately for the different groupings of assets, but you would make only a single entry to the depreciation expense account.

Accounting for Sales of Capital Assets

There are two ways to account for the sale of a capital asset. In the end, it really does not matter which method you use, because in any case, you will have to do it a different way for tax purposes.

When you have several assets in a group, it can be difficult to determine the undepreciated cost related only to a particular asset. For example, if you purchased a desk three years ago and posted it to the furniture and fixtures account, how do you know how much has been depreciated? It is possible to find the original cost from your capital asset sub-ledger and recalculate the depreciation. You would then remove those amounts from the books. Here is a more concrete example:

Desk:

Original cost	**$1,200.00**
A/D	**720.00**
Sales proceeds	**500.00**

The entry to record the sale would look like this:

DR	**Cash**	**$500.00**	
DR	**A/D: furniture**	**720.00**	
CR	**Furniture**		**$1,200.00**
CR	**Gain on sale**		**20.00**

You can see that this entry accounts for the cash you got in the door, removes the value in the asset and A/D accounts related to the desk, and records the fact that you made $20 on the sale.

An easier although less accurate method is to simply record the $500 as a reduction to the asset account. What this means is that the gain on the sale won't be recognized until every asset has been sold out of the grouping, which may never happen. As long as the gains and losses are not large, this second method is adequate. The entry to record the sale would then be —

DR	**Cash**	**$500.00**	
CR	**Furniture**		**$500.00**

CASE STUDY

As always, Vivian put Becky's mind at ease. Becky was definitely on the right track. All of the costs of the generator, including the electrician fees, the venting, and even the freight (Becky had forgotten about that) were to be included in the cost.

As for the depreciation method, Vivian explained that the easiest way was for Becky to use the same rates as were allowed for income tax purposes. The generator was equipment and, as such, was depreciated using a declining balance rate of 20 percent. As was usual for tax purposes, only half of that depreciation could be taken in the year of purchase, so it would end up being depreciated 10 percent this year.

Becky was becoming more adept at moving around in the *QuickBooks* system, so Vivian let her input the capital asset balances and accumulated depreciation. All new assets, she explained, would be input directly into the software. At the end of the year, Becky would make the depreciation entries for each grouping of assets based on the rates that Vivian had provided her.

Chapter Summary

- Capital assets have value to the company in future years as well as the current year.
- Satellite costs should be capitalized along with the purchase cost of the asset.
- Depreciation is a method of bringing the cost of the asset into expenses over time.
- You generally recognize gains and losses on the sale of capital assets when there are no more assets in that category.

Chapter 12

Leases and Loans

In this chapter, you will learn —

- The difference between a lease and a loan
- The two major types of leases: capital and operating
- How to set up lease and loan transactions
- How to read an amortization schedule

In the course of business, there may be many loan transactions, including bank loans, loans from the company to other companies or individuals, and longer-term loans, such as the mortgage on the land and building in which the company operates. In addition, leases are becoming a prevalent way to finance and have the use of equipment and vehicles.

The accounting behind leases and loans can be a bit difficult to navigate. Most loans are set up as a fixed payment with a changing proportion of interest and principal. Leases can be used as a way to get the use of an asset without owning it outright or can be another method of financing an asset. The accounting in each scenario differs.

This chapter looks at equipment and vehicle leases and their treatment for accounting purposes, then moves on to a discussion of loans.

Lease Transactions: An Overview

Leasing is one way for companies of all sizes to have the use of assets. The entity that is providing the asset is called the lessor. The entity receiving the asset is called the lessee. Most capital assets, from vehicles to computers to machinery, can be leased.

Leases fall into two major categories: operating and capital. As GAAP can vary from country to country, you should discuss leasing with your accountant. This chapter presents US and Canadian GAAP with respect to leases.

CASE STUDY

Becky showed Vivian the lease documents she and Joe had signed three months ago for the new compressor. All Becky knew was that they were paying $259 a month for 36 months and that they could buy it at the end of the lease.

"Well, don't I just record the lease payments as an expense?" asked Becky. "After all, I have to either buy it or give it back in three years."

"We need to look at the documents and find out more information," Vivian explained. "There are two types of leases — capital and operating — and they are accounted for quite differently."

Becky said, "I was afraid you were going to say that!"

An operating lease simply reflects the fact that you are renting the use of an asset. It is usually a short-term lease that can be canceled. The lessee has neither the risks nor the rewards of ownership. If the asset breaks down, the lessor has to fix it, not the lessee. If it increases in value, the lessor gets the benefit, not the lessee.

Most office space rentals are structured this way. You rent the office space for the term of the lease, then you have to leave. The space doesn't belong to you.

Most vehicle leases are also structured this way. You are basically "renting" the vehicle for the term of the lease, then you either have to buy it at its fair market value or give it back. You do not own it.

A capital lease, however, represents a method of financing an asset, similar to a loan. The lessee makes payments for the lease period, after which time, the lessee either owns the asset outright or can buy it for a nominal amount. During the lease period, the lessee must insure the asset and finance any repairs or maintenance required. The lessee therefore has taken on the risks and rewards of ownership.

There are three criteria that are used to determine if a lease counts as a capital lease. Only one of these criteria must be met:

1. The lease term is equal to 75 percent or more of the estimated useful life of the asset.
2. The present value of the lease payments is equal to 90 percent or more of the value of the asset at the beginning of the lease.
3. The lease transfers ownership of the asset to the lessee at the end of the lease term or allows the lessee to purchase the asset at a bargain price (referred to as a bargain purchase option).

Although these conditions seem difficult to understand and follow, they are used only to ascertain whether or not the lessee actually controls the asset during the lease period. If so, the lessee is required to treat the asset as if the lessee bought it.

Accounting for Operating Leases

From a bookkeeping perspective, operating leases are the easy ones to handle. The periodic lease payment is simply treated as an expense of the period in which it is paid. For example, if the lease payment were $350 per month (ignoring taxes), the entry would be —

DR	**Equipment lease**	**$350.00**	
CR	**Bank**		**$350.00**

There would be no assets or liabilities set up on the balance sheet, even though an asset exists along with a liability to make payments for the term of the lease. This is called "off-balance sheet" financing.

Accounting for Capital Leases

In the case of a capital lease as determined by the criteria discussed above, the lessee is considered to have purchased the asset and has a corresponding liability to pay. This is similar to the treatment of loans.

Let's have a look at an example. A company leases machinery for a lease period of 30 months. The lease payments are $300 per month for the 30 months, after which the company can buy the equipment for $1. The estimated value of the equipment is $750 after three years.

This lease is a capital lease because of the bargain purchase option. The lessee is almost guaranteed to buy out the lease at the end of the term because the equipment is worth more ($750) than what has to be paid ($1).

A capital lease means you must treat the asset as if you purchased it. You therefore have to determine the value of the equipment. The value of the equipment is the present value of the lease payments. (Stay with me; it's not as nasty a concept as it seems.)

If you were the lessee in the example above, you would have to pay $300 per month for 30 months; however, this payment would include interest: let's say 12 percent annual interest (or 1 percent per month). Therefore, when you back out the interest portion, you get the total amount of principal payments on the lease. It's like a backwards amortization table. (Amortization tables are discussed later in this chapter.) You can figure out the principal portion of a lease by using a present value of annuity table. The relevant section of such a table for this example is —

Period	Discount Rate		
	1%	2%	3%
28	24.316	21.281	18.764
29	25.066	21.844	19.188
30	**25.808**	22.396	19.600

When we take the monthly payment and multiply it by the factor in the table, we get:

$300 X 25.808 = $7,742.40

The accounting to reflect this capital lease is —

DR	**Capital assets**	**$7,742.40**	
CR	**Capital lease obligations (liability)**		**$7,742.40**

Once the value of the asset is determined using the present value table, an amortization schedule can be developed to determine how much of the monthly payments represents principal repayments and how much represents interest expense. The entry to account for the monthly payment would look like this:

DR Capital lease obligations

DR Interest

CR Bank

CASE STUDY

Vivian quietly worked through the calculations while Becky watched. Finally, she spoke: "Well, it's a capital lease."

"How did you determine that?" asked Becky, staring at the lease agreement.

"I applied three criteria to the lease agreement. The first criterion is whether or not the lease term is 75 percent or more of the useful life of the asset. The useful life of this compressor is about five years, and your lease term is for 30 months, so you are leasing it for only 50 percent of its useful life. The lease does not meet the first criterion. Then I looked at the second criterion: whether or not the present value of the lease payments equals 90 percent or more of the value of the asset. At the 12 percent interest in the lease contract, the present value of the lease payments is $6,684. If you were to buy the compressor outright, it would cost you $8,000. That means the present value of the lease payments is less than the required 90 percent of the value of the asset."

"So, it's an operating lease, then," Becky said, her impatience with the numbers visible.

"Not quite. The lease allows you to buy the compressor at the end of 30 months for $25, though the lease states the fair market value is $350. This counts as a bargain purchase option, and therefore makes the lease a capital lease. Let's get it set up on the balance sheet."

Accounting for Loans

Loans are a little more straightforward than leases. You do not have to worry about the type of loan because every loan is used to finance business assets or operations.

There are two main types of loans: those with fixed payments that have differing interest and principal components, and those with fixed principal repayments and a floating interest component.

Let's start with the easy type first: those with fixed principal repayments. For example, let's say the original loan is for $20,000 at 5 percent interest for a five-year term. Repayment terms stipulate that you have to pay back principal of $333.33 per month, plus interest. In the books, the setup for the initial loan would look like this:

DR	**Cash**	**$20,000.00**	
CR	**Loan payable**		**$20,000.00**

This entry records the reality of the situation. You have debited cash because you now have $20,000 in loan proceeds sitting in your bank account. You also have a liability to pay off the $20,000 over the next five years. Note that this loan would be set up in the long-term liabilities section of your ledger because it will last longer than 12 months.

In this example, the loan is advanced by the bank at which you have your business account. Every month, your bank will withdraw from your account the $333.33 principal repayment and the interest. The interest will drop every month as the principal amount decreases. In the first month, the bank takes out —

Principal	**$333.33**
Interest	**83.33**

The accounting entry to record this is —

DR	**Loan payable**	**$333.33**	
DR	**Interest expense**	**83.33**	
CR	**Bank**		**$416.66**

It's important to remember that the loan liability balance will decrease only by the principal portion of the payment. The interest portion is recorded as an expense of the period in which the payment is made.

The second type of loan is a loan with fixed — usually monthly — payments. These payments are blended: a portion is principal and a portion is interest. Most mortgages are set up this way. To determine how much belongs to each category, you must look at an amortization table.

An amortization table calculates interest based on the terms of the loan and allocates the rest of the fixed payment to principal. Because the interest portion will decrease with every payment (it's being calculated on a decreasing loan balance), the principal portion will increase.

The easiest way to obtain an amortization schedule is to ask your lender to provide one. This way, you know that the amounts set out in the table will match your actual payments exactly. If your lender is unwilling or unable to provide you with an amortization table, you will have to create one yourself. Go to www.numbers101.com to find an amortization calculation tool to help you with this task.

The entry to record the payment is the same as the entry for the first type of loan (fixed principal repayments) described above. However, the interest and principal in the entry will change with each payment. You will find the split between principal and interest by using the amortization table and apportion the payment accordingly.

The entry to record a payment on the table would be —

DR Loan payable

DR Interest expense

CR Bank

Reconciling the Loan Balance

Although following the amortization tables should produce the correct loan balance for you at the end of the year, it's a good idea to double-check your balance against the loan statement you receive from your bank. If your bank doesn't produce a loan statement, verbal confirmation from them is fine.

If your balance differs from the bank balance, first check to make sure you have recorded all of the entries from the amortization table. If you have, and your balance and the bank's still differ, ask your bank to print off the activity on the loan for the year. Compare the print off to what you have posted and work with the bank and your accountant to find the differences.

Chapter Summary

- Leasing is becoming a common way for small businesses to have control over assets.
- There are two major types of leases: operating and capital.
- A lease must meet at least one of three criteria to be a capital lease.
- Loan and capital lease repayments must be split between principal and interest payments.

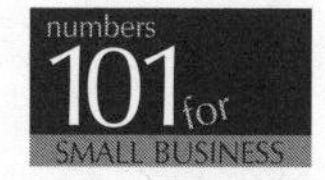

Chapter 13

Transactions between the Company and Its Owners

In this chapter, you will learn —

- How to account for shareholder loans
- How to track business expenses for which you pay personally
- What happens when the company uses personal assets
- How to account for bonuses and dividends

As a small-business owner, you will have many interactions with your business finances, especially in the start-up phase. Sometimes, you might be short on personal cash, so you buy groceries with the company debit card. You may be out at a store and see a phenomenal deal on office supplies but have only personal cash, so you buy the supplies, knowing that the company will pay you back later.

Although these are common transactions, it's wise to minimize this type of activity. For one thing, it creates more bookkeeping (and you don't need any more bookkeeping than you already have!). Second, if your company were to be audited by the IRS or CRA or other taxation bodies, they would find that you have created a link between your business and your personal finances. You may have accounted for all of these transactions correctly, but the fact that you've mixed personal and business finances may cause the government to dig a little deeper to make sure you are not deducting personal expenses for tax purposes. A hassle all around!

Nonetheless, there will be times when you have no choice. This chapter looks at shareholder loans, business use of personal assets, and bonuses and dividends.

Shareholder Loans

The phrase "shareholder loans" implies that you are a corporation. If your business is

CASE STUDY

Becky was confused. Vivian was asking her which personal assets she and Joe owned but used partly for the business.

"Well, we have the office and the shop here at the house," she said. "Joe's truck is in his name but it's used only for business."

"What about your car?" Vivian asked.

"I use it to go to the bank and to buy office supplies, I suppose," she said. "And I pick up customer checks sometimes," she added.

"Anything else?" Vivian prompted.

"Hmm. Well, the computer is mine. We use it mostly for business but we've never accounted for it before."

Vivian smiled. "Let's sit down and make a list of all the things the business uses that belong to you and Joe personally."

unincorporated, the concept still applies, but you will track these transactions in your equity account instead of a loan account.

The shareholder account is set up on your balance sheet as a liability account, but it could have either a positive or a negative balance. If it has a debit balance, it is an asset to the company. It means that you owe the company money.

The following transactions will debit the shareholder loan account:

- The company pays for a personal expense.
- You draw money out of the company and intend to pay it back.
- You account for personal use of a company-owned vehicle.

The following transactions will credit the shareholder account:

- You spend your own money on business expenses.
- The company owes you a bonus or dividends but hasn't paid them out to you yet.
- You account for the business use of personal assets.

It's important to keep control over the balance of your shareholder loan account. In most tax jurisdictions, running a debit balance (i.e., you owe the company money) carries tax implications. Were it not for these rules, company owners could keep "borrowing" from their companies instead of taking a salary, thereby paying no income tax. Your accountant can help you avoid this minefield.

Now, let's look at some of the common shareholder transactions.

You Pay for a Business Expense out of Your Own Pocket

There will probably be times when you have to pick up the tab for a business expense. There may be no funds in the business account, or you might have forgotten the business credit card at home when you went out to the store.

Because these transactions do not appear in the business bank account, it is easy to forget them; and in fact, I see this happen a lot. There are two really good reasons why you need to pay attention and track these expenses. First, it's money that the company owes you tax-free. You do not have to pay tax on expense reimbursements. Second, the company still gets to deduct these expenses on the tax return, even though you paid them out of your own pocket. Think of it this way: For every receipt worth one dollar that you don't claim but leave sitting in your pocket or purse, you have thrown away at least 25 cents. Claim the expense. Get the deduction.

The accounting for this type of transaction looks like this:

DR	**Office expense**	**$100.00**	
DR	**Retail tax liability**	**7.00**	
CR	**Shareholder loan**		**$107.00**

It is identical to the transaction you would record if you bought the item out of the business account, except you're crediting the shareholder loan instead of cash. Make sure that you keep the invoice or receipt the same way you would for any other business expense. You have simply paid for it out of your pocket instead of out of the bank.

The Company Pays for a Personal Expense

This is the opposite of the transaction described above. You may be short of personal funds and need to use company funds. It's important to track the business cash outlay, but you want to make sure that you are not expensing the item in the books of the business, because the expense is not business related.

The accounting looks like this:

DR	**Shareholder loan**	**$107.00**	
CR	**Cash**		**$107.00**

Notice that you ignore the tax component of the transaction as well. The tax paid on personal expenses is not recoverable. This transaction simply says that money went out of the company and that the shareholder owes the company for it.

What Happens If I Run My Business out of My House?

Many small businesses are run out of a portion of the owner's house, such as the basement or spare bedroom. It's only fair that the business should pay for a portion of the costs of running your home.

You need to be careful here. Some owners who do not want to be bothered to calculate utilities and other expenses just charge a flat rent to the company. This tactic puts them on dangerous tax ice, as they have now created rental income for themselves personally. If they don't want to be taxed on all that money, they will have to calculate utilities and other expenses anyway to deduct from that income. It's better to bite the bullet and realize that calculating how much it costs you to run your business from your home will take a bit of time. Keep it as a simple reimbursement of actual expenses, and your life will be much easier!

Here's a simple two-step process to help you calculate how much of your home expenses you can assign to your business.

Step 1: How much space?

To figure out how much of the expenses belongs to the business, you need to calculate how much space the business takes up in the house. First, calculate the entire square footage of the living spaces of the house. Living spaces do not include unfinished basements or attics or unheated garages or outbuildings. This may sound obvious, but make sure that you include the space that the business occupies in the calculation. For example, if your basement is mostly unfinished, but your office takes up a 10-foot by 10-foot space in the only finished part of the basement, make sure you are including that one hundred square feet in your total.

Once you have calculated the total square footage of the house, you need to calculate the square footage of the office area. Start by measuring the rooms used only for business. If you have a room that is never used for anything but business, calculate the square footage of that room (multiply the length times the width). Next, look at the rooms that are used partly for business. This area gets a little gray so you may want to discuss it with your accountant. Let's look at a couple of examples so you know what I mean.

- A side entrance and hallway leads directly into your office space and is never used to get to other parts of the house. This area would be considered business square footage.
- A dining room is used for business seven hours a day and for family meals and activities the rest of the time. This area needs to be split by usage. For example, if the dining room is 10 feet by 12 feet, the total square footage is 120. However, the room is used only for business purposes seven hours a day. The business square footage is therefore 120 X 7/24 = 35 square feet.
- Once you've calculated the business square footage, you will know how much of the house the business takes up. For example, if the house is 2,000 square feet, and the total business usage is 250 square feet, you would arrive at the percentage of the house the business takes (the business percentage) up by the following calculation: 250/2,000 = 12.5%.

Step 2: Calculating the expenses

Which household expenses should the business share with you? Here are some of the common operating costs of a home:

- Property taxes
- Heat
- Electricity
- Water
- Mortgage interest
- Repairs and maintenance
- Home insurance

Even if you rent your home or apartment, you can apportion a part of your rent expense to the business.

Total up all your expenses, then multiply by the business percentage. That's all there is to it.

Repairs and maintenance expense requires some discussion here. There are four categories of repairs, and each is handled differently.

Capital improvements

If you build an addition to your house, build interior walls, or pave a previously unpaved driveway, you are making capital improvements. These things ultimately increase the value of your house.

You do not take capital improvements into your calculation of repairs and maintenance for your business, because there are income tax implications to doing so in many jurisdictions, that the discussion of which are beyond the scope of this book. Ask your accountant.

Repairs that affect the whole house

Some examples of these types of repairs are duct cleaning, water-softener repair, roof repairs, and lawn cutting. These expenses relate to the business square footage as well as your personal square footage. These repairs and maintenance expenses will be prorated based on square footage, just as your other house expenses are.

Repairs that affect only the personal square footage

Expenses such as repainting your master bedroom or fixing the plumbing in the upstairs bathroom in no way relate to the business use of the house. You would therefore not use any of these types of expenses in your calculations.

Repairs that affect only the business square footage

Expenses such as laying carpet in or repainting your home office space relate only to business usage. You can take 100 percent of these expenses into your calculation. You do not have to prorate these expenses based on square footage.

The accounting entry to set up the home office expense in the corporation is —

DR Home office expenses

CR Shareholder loan

This entry reflects the expense in the company and also that the company owes you for its portion of those expenses. Note that if your expenses carry a recoverable sales tax component (such as GST in Canada), you would also debit the sales tax recoverable account so that you will get back the tax you paid on those expenses.

Here's a concrete example of a home office calculation:

Total square footage of house		1,450 square feet
Square footage of office space		225 square feet
Heat	$1,250.00	
Electricity	1,612.00	
Property taxes	1,750.00	
Mortgage interest	9,849.00	
Roof repair	2,950.00	
Hot tub repair (master bedroom)	615.00	
Paint for office space	95.00	

What is the home office expense for the year? Ignore taxes.

Prorated expenses (1,250 + 1,612 + 1,750 + 9,849 + 2,950) X 225/1,450 =	$2,701.71
Personal expenses 0% (615)	0.00
Business expenses 100% (95)	95.00
Total home office expense	$2,796.71

Your entry would be —

DR Home office expense	**$2,796.71**	
CR Shareholder loan		**$2,796.71**

Hey, the Business Uses My Car Too!

Many small business owners use vehicles registered in their own names for business purposes. In most cases, doing so is actually better from a tax perspective than having a car in the company's name and using it personally part of the time.

If you use your own vehicle in the business, you need to make sure the business pays its fair share of the costs. The calculation is similar to the home office expense but it is based on miles driven. There are two common ways of calculating business vehicle usage. Both are described below. Your ability to use one or the other depends on the tax rules in your jurisdiction. (You know the drill: talk to your accountant.)

Business mileage

Both methods require that you track the number of miles (or kilometers) you drove for business purposes in the year. The easiest way to do this is to keep a mileage log in your glove box. Whenever you are on business, jot down the date, where you're going, and how many miles you covered. If you do a regular bank run or something similarly repetitive, it is sufficient to track the miles on that trip once and use that standard number for each trip to the same place.

Not only will a mileage log help you calculate your business vehicle expenses, it also provides you with back up if you are audited. It's one way to prove that you actually drove all of those miles for business.

One thing to note here is that in most tax jurisdictions, the daily trip from your home to your office (assuming you do not have a home office) is considered personal mileage, not business mileage. (Go figure!) You would therefore not include this amount in your business calculation.

Method 1

This is the simpler of the two methods. Let's assume that you drove 5,000 miles for business purposes in a year. You would multiply this figure by the per-mile rate allowed by the IRS. (These rates change frequently, so check with the IRS for the current rate.) For example, if the rate was 0.67 per mile, your vehicle expense would therefore be —

5000 X 0.67 = $3,350

Canadian readers will have to check with CRA for the current per-kilometer rate. Let's say that it's 0.39, and you drove 7,000 kilometers per year for business purposes. Your calculation would be —

7000 X 0.39 = $2,730

Method 2

This method takes longer to calculate but is more accurate. If you have had significant repairs done on the vehicle during the year, this calculation will probably yield more expense.

You start the same way as the previous method: by calculating business mileage. In this method, however, you will also need to calculate the total mileage on the vehicle for the year. In keeping with our example, let's say that the vehicle was used on company business for the same 5,000 miles (or kilometers) per year. The total miles (or kilometers) the vehicle was driven is 10,000. The business, therefore, accounts for 50 percent of the vehicle's total usage.

The second step is for you to calculate the actual expenses incurred for the vehicle; for example, fuel, insurance, license fees, repairs, lease costs, or financing interest. Then you simply add up these costs and multiply them by the business-use percentage (which, in the above example, was 50 percent).

A third step involves depreciation on the vehicle. The per-mile or per-kilometer rates in the first method take depreciation into consideration. When you're dealing with actual expenses, you need to calculate the depreciation.

When you first begin using your vehicle for business purposes, you need to assess a rough market value at that point. You do this because, in a sense, you are "selling" the business a portion of your vehicle, even though you are not transferring title. You set up this value as your depreciable value. (See Chapter 11 for a more full discussion of depreciable assets.) You then apply the applicable depreciation percentage against the value to arrive at your total depreciation expense. Finally you apply the business-use percentage to the total depreciation expense to get the business depreciation expense. I know it sounds complicated, but it's really fairly easy. Here's an example:

Vehicle value at start date of business	$14,000.00
Business miles (or kilometers)	2,938
Total miles (or kilometers)	12,475
Depreciation rate	30%

Total depreciation:
$14,000.00 X 30% = $4,200.00

Business depreciation:
$4,200.00 X 2,938/12,475 = $989.15

Therefore, $989.15 is the amount of depreciation that becomes part of the business vehicle expense.

What about Other Personal Assets Used for Business?

There are some other common personal assets or expenses that you might use partly for your business, such as your home computer, your cell phone, your land line, or your Internet connection.

Any asset worth more than $200 (such as your home computer) would be depreciated much like your personal vehicle. You would find the value of the asset at the time you started using it for business purposes, depreciate it (use the tax rates for simplicity), and calculate the company's portion of the depreciation. For example, if the total depreciation is $450, and the company uses the computer half of the total time it is used, then the company gets $225 in depreciation expense. The company also owes you this money.

For any personal expenses, such as your phone lines and Internet connection, you would simply split the cost according to usage.

Caveat

The treatment of personal assets used in a business varies substantially from case to case. If you were to ask ten accountants how

CASE STUDY

Becky couldn't believe it. "You mean, we could have deducted all these expenses from our income taxes for the business?"

"Absolutely. And we will," Vivian added. "We'll go back and refile your taxes for the past three years. From now on you need to track those expenses on an ongoing basis."

"Right. I'll keep a mileage log for my car in the glove box and make sure I write down all the trips I make for the business. I'll keep all the gas and repair receipts in the glove box, too." Becky started making notes for herself.

"And don't forget to keep all the utility receipts for the house. You can claim a percentage of those as well." Vivian shook Becky's hand. It had been a long day, and both women were tired.

"I'll stop by next week and see how everything is coming along." As Vivian turned to go, Becky threw her arms around the accountant and hugged her. "Thank you so much for helping us out of this mess," she said.

Vivian smiled as she left.

they do it, they'll most likely give you 11 answers. What we have discussed above is a general framework for how to deal with these issues. Because tax law varies between jurisdictions, it's important to discuss these issues with your tax accountant. Once your accountant gives you the structure to follow, you can proceed with confidence.

Setting up the Management Bonus

As the boss of the company, you have many options regarding how you can take remuneration from the company.

If you are not incorporated, you may draw whatever is available or nothing at all. It doesn't matter, because you will be taxed on the net income before draws.

If you are incorporated, however, you have to plan your remuneration more carefully. Chapter 22 goes into the issues surrounding shareholder remuneration more fully. This section will discuss the accounting for the bonus accrual.

At the end of its fiscal year, the company may accrue a management bonus to the owner/manager for tax reasons. This bonus is not actually paid yet, but it is allowed as a deduction for the company's income taxes. The gross amount of the bonus gets set up as both an expense to the company and as an amount owing to the shareholder. The entry looks like this:

DR Management bonus expense

CR Management bonus payable

Some companies credit the shareholder loan account instead, but it is a good idea to segregate the bonus into a separate account so that you remember to deduct withholdings when the amount is actually paid out. Payroll taxes are not taken into consideration until the bonus is actually paid out to you, because payroll taxes are expenses for the period during which the bonus is paid.

For example, if a bonus of $25,000 is declared, the entry at the end of the fiscal year is —

DR Management bonus expense **$25,000.00**

CR Management bonus payable **$25,000.00**

If, a month later, you want to pay $5,000 gross from this bonus, your entry would look something like this:

DR Management bonus payable	**$5,000.00**	
DR Payroll tax expense	**212.00**	
CR Payroll tax liability		**$1,425.00**
CR Cash		**3,787.00**

The debit to the payroll tax expense reflects the company's share of the payroll taxes that must be remitted. The credit to the payroll tax liability reflects both the company's payroll taxes and the employee's withholdings. This entry tells you that the company paid out $5,000 of the $25,000, and some of that went to you (the employee) and some went to the government.

Dividends

The tax and planning issues associated with declaring and paying dividends are also discussed in more detail in Chapter 22. Here we will look at the accounting for the dividend.

Dividends are handled a little differently than bonuses, because dividends are paid out of retained earnings, not current income. The dividend account should be set up in the equity section instead of the expense section.

A company first declares a dividend payable. All this means is that the company prepares a little paperwork saying that the directors have agreed that dividends will be paid to the shareholders of the company. (If you are a one-person show, you will be both a director and a shareholder.)

There are a couple of important points to note here. First, like the management bonus accrual, the dividend is set up in the books of the company when it is declared, not when it is paid. Second, the dividend affects only the balance sheet, and never the income statement.

The entry to record the dividend accrual is —

DR Dividends (in the equity section)

CR Shareholder loan

It's not as important to segregate the liability to pay dividends, because there are no withholding tax implications. When the dividend is actually paid, the shareholder loan is debited and cash credited.

Chapter Summary

- If your business is incorporated, the transactions between you and the company are shareholder loans. If your business is unincorporated, these transactions affect owner's equity.
- When the company uses a personal asset of the owner, the expenses must be apportioned between business use and personal use.
- Management bonuses are an expense to the company.
- Dividends are not an expense; they are paid out of retained earnings.

Chapter 14

Remittances to the Government

In this chapter, you will learn —

- What government remittances are
- How to manage the accounting for remittance liability accounts
- Which taxes a US company must withhold
- Which taxes a Canadian company must withhold
- How to reconcile the remittance accounts

This chapter looks at the money that your company must collect on behalf of the government in day-to-day transactions and which it must remit to the government on a periodic basis. This issue gets many small businesses into trouble. Let's start with a few critical warnings about government remittances:

1. *This money is not yours.* Do not spend it! Although this seems self-explanatory, thousands of small businesses all over the world get into serious trouble this way. It can be easy to forget that most of the $5,000 you have in your bank account belongs to the government, and to use it for "a little while" for short-term financing. Along comes the filing and remitting deadline, and you don't have the money anymore. So you don't file anything. Now, not only do you owe the remittance, you also owe interest and penalties. Further non-filing or non-payment results in your business bank accounts being frozen. Not a good scenario.

   The easy solution is to put the money aside, perhaps even in a separate bank account. Don't look at it; don't think about it. Just remit it when the time comes.
2. Make sure you reconcile your liability account in your books to

CASE STUDY

Becky never had an issue with payroll withholdings. Joe's Plumbing was a partnership, and as such, Joe and Becky took draws rather than paychecks. But sales tax always baffled her.

She wasn't sure that she was remitting the right amounts to the government. They had never been audited — which was a good thing — but she had a sneaky feeling that she wasn't deducting everything she was supposed to be deducting from the amount owing.

She pulled out her file of all the remittances for the past year in anticipation of Vivian's return.

what you're actually remitting to the government. It's easy to just concentrate on the changes in the account for the current period and forget that last period's amount did not get cleared out properly. Reconciliation will be discussed later in this chapter.

3. Keep good accounting records. You are holding this money in trust for the government, which will want to know that you have a handle on how much you owe. The government may also periodically want to see your source documents to make sure you're withholding the right amounts from your employees and that you're charging the right amount of tax to your customers. Document, document, document!

What Are Government Remittances?

There are two major categories of money you must collect on behalf of governments: employee withholdings and retail sales tax. At this point, I'm going to break out the differences between Americans and Canadians to show you that even though the taxes themselves are different, the concepts are the same.

US Remittances to the Government

The US has only one basic type of remittance: employment taxes (a similar concept to payroll taxes in Canada; see below). Currently, there is no federal sales tax.

Employment taxes

In the US, most employers are required to withhold income taxes, social security tax, and medicare taxes from their employees' paychecks. They must also match the employee contribution to social security and medicare taxes and remit both. Employers must also calculate and remit federal unemployment tax to the IRS.

To track withholding taxes, your company should set up the following accounts:

- Wages (i.e., the employee's gross wages)
- Employment taxes (expense) (i.e., the employer's share of payroll taxes)
- Employment tax liabilities (i.e., withholdings from the employee's pay and the employer's share)

The accounting entry for this will look like this:

DR Wages

DR Employment taxes (expense)

CR Payroll liabilities

CR Cash

The treatment of federal unemployment tax is a little different. It is calculated in most cases as 0.8 percent of the first $7,000 of an employee's wage. The employer bears the burden of this tax; nothing is withheld from the employees' pay.

When it is time to remit this tax, you would set up the entry as —

DR Employment taxes (expense)

CR Cash

Some companies' bookkeeping systems automatically accrue the amounts owing for FUTA, but it is not necessary to do so.

State sales tax

Most states have their own forms of retail sales tax. A discussion of those taxes is beyond the scope of this book.

Other remittances to the government

There are several other remittances that you might have to make to various levels of government in the US, including state taxes. The concepts for these are the same as for the remittances we have already discussed.

Canadian Remittances to the Government

Payroll taxes

In Canada, employers are required to withhold employment insurance premiums (EI), Canada pension plan premiums (CPP), and federal and provincial income tax from their employees' gross pay. On top of that, the employer must remit their own premiums to EI and CPP. At the time of printing, an employer has to match the required CPP premium deducted from the employees' pay and has to pay 1.4 times the employees' EI premium.

In the books of the company, there would be several accounts set up to deal with this activity.

Wages (expense): The gross wages of the employee would go into this account.

Payroll taxes (expense): The employer's portions of the CPP and EI premiums go into this account.

Payroll liabilities: This account is for both the withholdings from the employees' pay and the employer's portion of the CPP and EI premiums.

Let's look at an example of how these remittances are accounted for. Say an employee makes $35 per hour and worked 80.25 hours in the pay period. Her gross pay would be $2,808.75. From the income tax tables provided by Canada Revenue Agency, the required CPP is $123.01, the required EI is $146.92, and the combined federal and provincial income tax is $842.63. This means that the employer also has to contribute $123.01 in CPP (1 times the employee contribution) and $205.69 in EI (1.4 times the employee contribution).

The only actual expense for the employer for the payroll taxes is the employer's share. The rest comes out of the employee's gross pay. The accounting entry to capture all of this information is —

DR	**Wages**	**$2,808.75**	
DR	**Payroll taxes**	**328.70**	
CR	**Payroll liabilities**		**$1,441.26**
CR	**Cash**		**1,696.19**

This entry reflects the gross pay of $2,808.75, the extra taxes the employer has to pay of $328.70, the total amount owed to the government of $1,441.26, and the actual paycheck that goes to the employee of $1,696.19.

When the remittance to the government is made (usually the following month), the entry is —

DR	**Payroll liability**	**$1,441.26**	
CR	**Cash**		**$1,441.26**

This entry wipes out the liability and reflects the check cut to the government.

Goods and Services Tax (GST)

The GST is collectible by most businesses that have revenues of more than $30,000 annually on their sales of products or the provision of services. A business collects GST from its customers and must remit it to Canada Revenue Agency minus any GST the company has paid on the goods and services it buys. For example, if a business bills a customer for installation of drywall, the company would also add 5 percent to the bill. It holds that money in trust for the government and then remits it quarterly or annually. On the flip side of the coin, the business also gets credit for all the GST it has paid on the things that it has purchased. For example, if the business buys office supplies for $100, it would have paid an additional $5 as GST. It can deduct that $5 from the GST it has to remit on its sales.

Generally, you will have to set up three accounts to handle the GST:

GST collected on sales: to accumulate the GST that your company charges to its customers

GST paid on purchases: to track the GST your company pays on all of its expenses

GST remitted: to account for the actual payments your company makes to the government

Let's look at a few examples:

1. Your company bills a customer $500 for website design. Your invoice is for $525 ($500, plus $25 in GST). The entry to record this is —

DR	**Accounts receivable**	**$525.00**	
CR	**Sales**		**$500.00**
CR	**GST collected on sales**		**25.00**

2. Your company pays $261.01 for office supplies. The receipt shows that $12.43 of this amount is GST. Your entry would be —

DR	**Office supplies**	**$248.58**	
DR	**GST paid on purchases**	**12.43**	
CR	**Accounts payable**		**$261.01**

3. Let's assume that there are no other GST transactions in the period. You are ready to prepare your remittance to Canada Revenue Agency. The total amount of GST that you are required to remit is $12.57 ($25.00 minus $12.43). Your entry would be —

DR	**GST remitted**	**$12.57**	
CR	**Cash**		**$12.57**

This still leaves amounts in the GST collected and the GST paid accounts. To clear theses amounts, you would make the following entry:

DR	**GST collected**	**$25.00**	
CR	**GST paid**		**$12.43**
CR	**GST remitted**		**12.57**

Some bookkeepers do this clearing entry every remittance cycle, and

CASE STUDY

"You're right, Becky, there are some problems with your remittances," Vivian said, leafing through the pile. "Your bookkeeping software will help you keep much better track of these taxes from now on."

"What was I doing wrong?" Becky asked, frowning.

"It looks like you were including only the expenses that you had the invoices for when you filed the returns. Here's an example," Vivian said, as she pointed to a remittance form. "In July, you filed the return for the period of April to June. But it looks like you received some more invoices in August that were dated in June. You should have claimed the taxes you paid on your next remittance, but it looks like you didn't, probably because you were looking only for invoices dated July to September at that point. You will be able to reconcile the net liability in the new software so you shouldn't have this problem any more."

"Can we go back and fix the old remittances?" Becky asked, disturbed that she had cost the business more money.

"Absolutely. Let's start correcting those."

some only at year-end. It's really up to you. My preference is at year end so that it is easy to see how much has been remitted year to date.

Other remittances to the government

Most provinces in Canada have their own provincial retail sales taxes. In some provinces, these are integrated with the federal GST, and in other provinces, the taxes are administered separately. The issues are similar to GST; however, in some provinces, instead of getting back the tax you pay, you simply do not pay the tax up front if you are registered. The complexities of provincial commodity taxation are beyond the scope of this book.

Reconciling the Remittance Accounts

As with any account on the balance sheet, you always need to be able to make sense of the numbers. For example, if your payroll tax liability account says that you owe $12,410, but you know that you are not behind in your remittances and the remittance for the last month is $1,747, you should be able to tell at a glance that something is wrong. Here are some troubleshooting tips for finding problems with the remittance accounts:

- Print out a detailed listing of the transactions in the remittance accounts. If you are on a manual system, scan the general journal in the appropriate remittance column. Make sure that you can find a remittance entry for each period you actually made a payment. For payroll liabilities, it's likely to be monthly (so there should be 12 entries for the year). In Canada, for GST, it's likely to be quarterly (so there should be four entries for the entire year). If there are fewer remittance entries than expected, it's possible that you have put the remittance entry in the wrong account. Retrace your entries.

- If there are the right number of entries but there's still a balance left over, group the transactions by remittance period. For example, you would look at each GST period for which you made a remittance. Does the difference between the GST collected for the period and the GST paid for the period equal the amount that you remitted? If not, you may have made a mathematical error in calculating your remittance, in which case, you will need to correct the remittance. Another possibility is that after you remitted for that period, you posted an entry into that period. To avoid this situation, ensure that your bookkeeping for that period has been completed and the bank account reconciled before you calculate the remittance.
- Check the balance owing on your books against the statements you receive from the government. Do they match? If not, the government may have posted one or more of your payments incorrectly. Or you may have forgotten to actually send in the remittance. Look into the accounting detail and track down the source of the problem.

Chapter Summary

- ➡ The two major types of remittances are payroll withholding taxes and retail sales taxes.
- ➡ You are holding these taxes in trust for the government. Do not spend that money!
- ➡ There are different types of remittances required in each jurisdiction, but the concepts are generally the same.
- ➡ It's important to reconcile your remittance accounts and keep good accounting records to track the amounts withheld.

Chapter 15

Maintaining a Petty Cash System

In this chapter, you will learn —

- What petty cash funds are for
- How to set up an imprest (i.e., reconciled) petty cash system
- How to reconcile your petty cash
- How to account for the petty cash items

Previous chapters have explained the importance of depositing all of your cash receipts into the bank account on a daily basis, and the importance of setting up a cash disbursement system for any payouts.

However, almost every business has a myriad of tiny expenses for which writing a check would be impractical: running to the store for coffee cream, for example, or getting stamps at the post office. Enter petty cash.

Petty cash is simply money kept on hand rather than deposited in the bank account. It can be kept in the cash register, an envelope, or a box for all of the occasions where you have an expense of only a few dollars. Although the petty cash fund is usually only $100 or so, it is important to keep control of the fund and to be able to reconcile it, both to make sure that all expenses have been accounted for and also to make sure that cash does not go missing. This chapter will show you how to set up, maintain, and replenish your petty cash system.

Setting up the Petty Cash Fund

To set up the fund initially, you will first have to decide where to keep it. It should either be in a cash register that is locked or in a lock box to which only one person has the key. It's critical to make only one person responsible for the petty cash fund to ensure that cash cannot go missing.

Once you have decided where it will be kept, you will write a check from your company bank account made payable to

CASE STUDY

"I have a half hour before my next appointment. I'll run out for stamps." Joe started for the door.

Joe returned 20 minutes later with stamps, a newspaper, and two coffees: one for Becky and one for himself.

"Wait a minute, pal, give me the receipts," Becky said. Joe rummaged around in his pants pocket and withdrew two crumpled receipts and deposited them on the desk. "Where's the coffee receipt?" Becky asked.

"They didn't give me one. All this came out of my own pocket anyway. Don't worry about it. You don't have to write it down."

Becky knew there had to be a better way to track all these tiny receipts that kept slipping through the cracks. She remembered Vivian's constant mantra, "If you don't save it, you can't claim it." She had no idea, however, how to set up a better system.

Becky added "Cash Expenses" to the list of issues to discuss with Vivian.

petty cash. Most businesses operate well with a $100 petty cash float. You can always increase it later if necessary.

You cash the check and put the money into the petty cash box. In your bookkeeping system, you would record the following transaction:

DR	**Petty Cash**	**$100**	
CR	**Bank**		**$100**

Using Your Petty Cash

Okay, you've set up your fund. Now how does it work? Every time you need funds for a small purchase (say, $3.14 for stamps), you would take the money out of petty cash. In this example, you might take a ten dollar bill out of petty cash when you go to the post office. When you return, you will have a receipt (remember, always get a receipt) for $3.14 and $6.86 in change. The combination of these two things is equal to the $10 you took out of the fund.

You will put the change and the receipt back into the box and record the date, amount, and type of transaction on your petty cash control sheet. Worksheet 2 is a petty cash control system you can use in your business.

One of the important features of the petty cash control sheet is that there is room at the bottom for summarizing the categories of transactions and for segregating the tax. These features will make it easier for you to enter the information into your bookkeeping system.

Once the actual cash in the petty cash fund gets low, you need to reconcile and replenish the fund.

Reconciling the Petty Cash Fund

Before you put more money in the fund, you first need to account properly for all the cash that has come out of the fund.

You start by totaling up and summarizing all the transactions on your petty cash control sheet. Your summary may look like this:

Worksheet 2
PETTY CASH CONTROL SHEET

Date:

Postage			Office Supplies			Miscellaneous		
Date	Expense	Tax	Date	Expense	Tax	Date	Expense	Tax
Total:			Total:			Total:		

Reconciliation:

Total expense and tax (Postage)	______________
Total expense and tax (Office Supplies)	______________
Total expense and tax (Miscellaneous)	______________
Total cash in box (counted)	______________
Minus: original petty cash	______________
Short/over	______________

CASE STUDY

"What's that?" Joe pointed to the shiny box he had noticed as soon as he came into the office.

"That's our new petty cash system," Becky said, patting the top of the box. "Vivian helped me set it up. From now on when you run out to get something, you'll take money from the box and you'll come back with receipts and the change from that money. That way, we'll be able to keep track of all these little expenses."

"I don't know, Becky. It sounds like a lot of work."

Becky, to her credit, refrained from hitting Joe. "Do you have any idea how much work it was for me the way we had it set up before?"

Joe chose his words carefully. "This new petty cash system sounds great. I'm sure I'll be able to adjust to the new way of doing things."

"I'm sure you will," Becky said, smiling.

Office supplies	$63.12
Postage	26.10
Miscellaneous	2.95
GST	5.25
Total	**$97.42**

It's easy to see that if you have $97.42 in expenses, there should be $2.58 left in cash in the box.

The reconciliation happens on the bottom of the petty cash control sheet. Start with the opening petty cash, subtract the expense receipts accounted for, and compare that number to what was actually counted in the box.

Opening petty cash	$100.00
Less: receipted expenses	97.42
Equals: Ending petty cash	2.58
Cash counted in box	2.58
Difference	0.00

If you end up being out of balance by more than a few cents, you will need to retrace your procedures and re-add the receipts.

Replenishing the Petty Cash Fund

At this point you need to top up the petty cash fund. You do this by writing a check for the exact amount of the total expenses; in the above example, $97.42. You cash this check and deposit the money into the box. Now you have the new $97.42 and the old $2.58, which once again totals $100.00.

Another way to think of the petty cash fund is that it will at any moment, between the receipts in the box and actual cash, total $100.00.

Now how do you record that check you just wrote? Well, you know the expenses that made up the $97.42. They are summarized on your petty cash control sheet. Our bookkeeping entry will be —

DR	**Office supplies**	**$63.12**	
DR	**Postage**	**26.10**	
DR	**Misc. expense**	**2.95**	
DR	**GST paid**	**5.25**	
CR	**Bank**		**$97.42**

Notice that the petty cash amount on your balance sheet will never change. It will always stay at $100.00 unless you make it larger.

I can't stress enough the importance of following these procedures for petty cash. Dealing with low-dollar-value receipts can be annoying, but unless they are tracked and properly accounted for, they could total up to a substantial amount of expenses that you are not claiming for income tax purposes. That's like throwing money off the balcony!

Chapter Summary

- The petty cash fund is used for small expenses for which it is impractical to write checks.
- Petty cash should be set up using an imprest system in which the total of receipts and cash left over always equals the original amount of petty cash.
- Petty cash needs to be reconciled frequently to ensure all receipts are accounted for and to prevent the disappearance of funds.
- The funds should be replenished monthly or when there is little money left in the fund.

Chapter 16

Reconciling the Bank

In this chapter, you will learn —

- What to do when your monthly bank statement comes
- How to reconcile your bank balance to your statement
- What to do if it doesn't work

Previous chapters have discussed the recording of most of your company's transactions to this point. Now you want to make sure that you have recorded everything that has actually gone through your company's bank account. You will do this in the reconciliation process. Most businesses get statements from the bank on a monthly basis, along with the canceled checks that have cleared the bank account. You may get your banking information more often than this if you have access to Internet banking. Some computerized bookkeeping programs allow you to download the bank information directly into the reconciliation module to assist in the process.

Although each computerized bookkeeping system has a different method for reconciling the books to the bank, this chapter will look at the manual process to give you a thorough understanding of the purpose of the exercise.

The Bank Statement Arrives

Life would be wonderful if you could open the envelope with your bank statement, compare the bank balance with the bank balance you have recorded in the general ledger, grunt happily when you see they are the same, then put away the bank statement and never look at it again.

Unfortunately, that rarely, if ever, happens. There are many reasons why the balance on your statement may not match the balance in your records.

Outstanding checks

It's quite possible that you have written and mailed checks that have not yet cleared the

CASE STUDY

"So, what is your process now when the bank statement comes?" Vivian asked Becky, sipping her coffee.

"I know I have to account for the bank charges, so I write them down. Then I file the bank statement away." Becky showed Vivian the bank statement that had come in the mail that morning.

"How do you know if you've recorded all the transactions?" asked the accountant.

"I know at the end of the year which receipts I've paid and which I haven't, so I know what checks I wrote. I don't need the bank statement to tell me that,"Becky said.

"What if the bank makes a mistake?" asked Vivian. "What if they put through a check twice or don't put one through at all? Wouldn't it be helpful to know that?"

Becky frowned. "I hadn't thought of that. I suppose you're going to show me a better way."

"That's my job," said Vivian, smiling.

bank. This would mean that your accounting balance in your ledger would show a decrease by the amount of those checks, but they would not yet be reflected by the bank. This difference is true and does not represent an error. It will be one of the items taken care of in the reconciliation process.

Outstanding deposits

You may also have situations where you have made a deposit at the bank on the last day of the month, but the bank processed it with the next business day's date on it. In this case, your ledger balance would be increased by the amount of the deposit but it would not yet be reflected in the bank statement. This is also an acceptable difference and will also be taken care of in the reconciliation process.

Bank charges

Banks usually charge interest and fees right at the end of the month, just before they print and mail you the statement. You may not know about these charges until you get your statement. You will need to record these bank charges in your ledger before you start the reconciliation process.

Automatic monthly payments

Your company may have leases or bank loans for which payments come out of the bank account automatically. You could account for these transactions during the month, or they may be left until the end of the month when the bank statement arrives. These transactions will need to be recorded in the journals before the reconciliation process can begin.

Bank errors

Yes, I know it's hard to believe, but your bank can make mistakes. Tellers can incorrectly record the amount of a check you wrote or a deposit you made or they can accidentally post someone else's transaction to your account. With the increase in bank computerization in recent years, the opportunities for human error are reduced, but such errors can still occur. Bank error is one of the important reasons for reconciling your account. Most banks will allow you to point out their error only for a certain amount of time, and after that time has elapsed, there may be nothing you can do about it. You must bring any bank error to the bank's attention immediately. It will be accounted for in the reconciliation process with the expectation that the bank will reflect the correction the following month.

The Reconciliation Process

All you are really doing in the bank reconciliation is explaining the differences between the bank balance on the statement and the bank balance in your ledger. As discussed above, there may be valid reasons why there are differences. They are called timing differences. You know, for example, that outstanding checks and deposits will be reflected by the bank in the next period.

Before you begin the reconciliation process, you must make sure that all other items that have correctly gone through your bank account have been accounted for in the general journal. There are two ways you can do this. You can tick off or highlight each entry in the general ledger that matches with an item on the bank statement. In accounting circles, this is called "ticking and bopping." (Don't ask me why. I didn't invent the terminology!)

A more efficient method is to perform a test reconciliation. You can look at your bank statement for the last few days of the year and see if you can identify checks or deposits that appear in your general journal but which don't appear on your statement. For example, if you wrote a batch of checks on October 31st and mailed them that day, you can bet that they will not appear on your October bank statement. There simply was not enough time for the check to have been delivered to your supplier, deposited by your supplier, and cleared through the bank's clearing system. In a test reconciliation, you would use these items that you know about to see if you can reconcile by including them in the calculation. If not, it's time to go back to ticking and bopping.

The format of a bank reconciliation is somewhat standard. Many bank statements will also have a reconciliation process on the back.

Sample 13 shows a typical bank reconciliation. Notice that the reconciliation starts with the balance from the bank statement and tries to get to the balance in the ledger. You would first subtract the outstanding checks (because they are already subtracted in your ledger), then add on the outstanding deposits (because they are included in your ledger). You then add or subtract any bank errors that you now know are going to be fixed by the bank next month. This process should give you a balance that matches your ledger balance. If it doesn't, you have to go back to your ticking and bopping process to find out where you went wrong.

As long as you have been careful, you can ignore those items that are ticked off or highlighted. We know that these items match. It is only the items that are not highlighted that you need to examine.

There are two types of items that may not match off: those that are on the bank statement and not in the ledger, and those that are in the ledger and not on the bank statement.

Sample 13
BANK RECONCILIATION

Small Company Inc.
Bank Reconciliation
31 December 2003

Balance per bank		**$18,412.97**
Less: outstanding checks		
#1457	(469.04)	
#1489	(12,432.12)	
#1505	(7,294.13)	(20,195.29)
Add: bank error		
#1451 taken out twice	936.85	936.85
Add: outstanding deposit	2,104.83	2,104.83
Balance per books		**$1,259.36**

Items on the bank statement that are not in the ledger

There will only ever be two categories of these entries: bank errors and bank entries that have not yet been accounted for. Bank errors will appear as a reconciling item on your bank reconciliation. Bank entries that you have not accounted for should be accounted for, and they can then be ticked off or highlighted with the corresponding bank statement entry. There should be no other items that are on your bank statement that are not in your ledger.

Items in your ledger that are not on your bank statement

There will only ever be two categories of these entries: bookkeeping errors and outstanding items (checks and deposits). You must correct bookkeeping errors before you start the reconciliation process. Outstanding items are accounted for in the reconciliation process.

What Happens If I Still Can't Reconcile?

Curse. Throw the ledger across the room. Have six beers. All of these things may temporarily make you feel better — I have tried all of these remedies and more! — but in the end, you still have to reconcile. Go back to the main purpose of what you are doing. You are looking at two lists of numbers and showing what the differences are.

There are some tried and true bookkeepers' shortcuts to finding certain types of errors. These are found in Chapter 17.

CASE STUDY

"I can't believe how easy that is," Becky said, marveling at the screen. "I can just download the bank information from the Internet, and the software does the matching for me."

"Yes. And then you are left with only those items that are different," said Vivian.

"I've already found a bank error. This check was written for $535.10 and the bank cashed it for $353.10. I'll have to call them right away about that."

"And don't forget to post that lease payment that you missed as well," Vivian said.

Becky said, "I don't think I would have caught that one with my old system. I'm so glad the bank is under control now!"

Example of the Bank Reconciliation Process

It's November 15th and your October bank statement comes in the mail. The relevant information is as follows:

- The automatic insurance payment that comes out of your account on the 12th of every month for $87.15 has not been accounted for in the books.
- There are bank charges of $17.65. These have not yet been reflected in the books.
- There are two outstanding checks that were written and mailed on October 31st: check 171 to your main supplier for goods ($1,595), and check 184 to the phone company ($127.43).
- You made a deposit on October 31st for $395.10 through your bank machine. It is posted in your account with a November 1st date.
- You notice that one of your checks was processed on your bank statement for the wrong amount. It should have been $941.12, and the bank posted it as $914.12.
- The October 31st bank balance on your bank statement is $4,375.14.
- The bank balance in your ledger is $3,125.61.

Step 1: Account for your month-end items

You must account for the insurance payment and the bank charges that are not yet in the books. Doing so will bring your ledger balance down to $3,020.81 ($3,125.61 – $87.15 – $17.65 = $3,020.81).

Step 2: Call the bank about the bank error

You may have to show the bank a copy of the canceled check to get them to correct the error, but you should make sure they are aware of it as soon as possible. This error ($27) will now be a reconciling item on your list.

Step 3: Attempt a test reconciliation

Now that you have accounted for those items that you know about, it's time to see if you can reconcile.

Your reconciliation will look like this:

Balance per bank		**$4,375.14**
Less: outstanding checks		
#171	(1,595.00)	
#184	(127.43)	(1,722.43)
Less: bank error		
Ck posted wrong amt	(27.00)	(27.00)
Add: outstanding deposit	395.10	395.10
Balance per books		**$3,020.81**

Hurray! It reconciles. No need for cursing, throwing, or excessive drinking. However, you can still find other reasons to do these things if you must.

Chapter Summary

- Reconciling your bank account is instrumental to ensuring that all of your transactions have been recorded.
- Reconciliation is the process of taking two numbers and explaining the difference between them.
- The balance on your bank statement and the balance in the ledger will be different by outstanding checks, outstanding deposits, and errors.
- Bank charges must be posted from the bank statement before you try to reconcile.

Chapter 17

When the Damn Thing Just Won't Balance

In this chapter, you will learn —

- The mechanics of reconciliation
- How to troubleshoot reconciliation problems
- Bookkeepers' tricks for zeroing in on the problem

No matter how great a bookkeeper you are, how many courses you've taken or how many years' experience you have, you will run into reconciliation problems that you just can't figure out. They will annoy you, drive you crazy (and possibly to drink), and cause you to use all kinds of colorful expressive language.

To solve these problems, you need to go back to the basics and answer the question, "What am I trying to do here?"

The Process of Reconciliation

The purpose of reconciliation, whether you are reconciling the bank account, credit card account, or other account balance, is simple. You have two numbers and you are explaining why they are not the same. If they are the same, they are automatically reconciled. When there are differences, you have to figure out why. Let's look at an example:

	List A	List B
	1,292	976
	370	47
	1,912	1,853
	47	1,292
	657	4,712
	4,306	657
	976	6,310
Total	**9,560**	**15,847**

The total of List A is 9,560, and the total for List B is 15,847. The balances are not the same, so you need to reconcile them.

You know that you care only about the differences. Numbers that are the same on both lists are not part of the difference. Take a highlighter and highlight the numbers that appear on both lists. You can ignore these numbers. All the unhighlighted numbers are part of the difference.

There are two pieces to the difference; the numbers that appear in List A that aren't on List B, and the numbers that appear on List B that aren't on List A.

You need to reconcile the List A balance to the List B balance. The general process you'll follow involves taking the List A balance, subtracting the numbers that are not on the List B balance, and adding in the numbers that are on the List B balance that aren't on the List A balance. This will give you your List B balance. The reconciliation would look like this:

List A balance		9,560
Less: items on List A not on List B		
	(370)	
	(1,912)	
	(4,306)	(6,588)
Add: items on List B not on List A		
	1,853	
	4,712	
	6,310	12,875
Total		15,847
List B balance		15,847
Difference		0

The second part of any reconciliation is, of course, to find out why the numbers do not match. However, in this section, you need only be concerned with identifying the numbers themselves.

Now, the above example looks easy and clear. But what if each list had dozens or hundreds of numbers? It would be a much more difficult process. If you follow the above procedure for your reconciliations and you still have an unidentified difference, there are a few bookkeepers' tricks to track down the source of the problem.

Backward Posting

One possibility is that as you are highlighting (or ticking and bopping) the numbers that match, one of the numbers is the same as on the other list, just the wrong way. For example, you may have a debit in List A of 1,240 and a credit in List B of 1,240 that you have inadvertently matched off against each other.

To see if you may have made this type of error, take the amount that you are still out by and divide by 2. Then look for that number in your list. In the above example, an error like that would have made you out by 2,480. You would divide that number by two to get 1,240 and would have found that number in both lists. Once you took a better look at those numbers, you would have discovered that one was posted backward, causing the out of balance.

Transposition Error

Transposition errors are another common bookkeeping error. They occur when two numbers are switched. For example, you may have wanted to write 57 but you wrote 75 instead.

Finding these errors is quite simple. They are always divisible by 9. In the above example, the difference between 57 and 75 is 18. Eighteen is divisible by 9.

You can also narrow down the magnitude of the error you are looking for. The difference above is 18. This tells you that the problem is in the tens column. If you made a transposition error by posting 8,312 instead of 3,812, the difference is 4,500, so you know the error is in the thousands column. This

CASE STUDY

No matter how hard she looked at the screen, Becky could not make the bank balance, even with the new software. She had downloaded the bank activity and had performed the auto match. Now the only things left to deal with were those her program showed her didn't match. She had investigated them one by one, making corrections as she came across posting errors and continued reconciling.

Somehow, she was still out by $270 even. Becky fixed herself another coffee, stared out at the falling snow for a few minutes, and came back at it with fresh eyes.

Vivian had worked through the first few reconciliations with her. This was the first one she was attempting on her own. She had worked through all the steps; had, in fact, even re-reconciled the prior month, just to prove she understood the technique.

Still out by $270. She threw the pen across the room, and it clattered against the window before dropping to the floor. The phone rang at the same instant, startling her. It was Vivian.

Becky barely allowed Vivian to say hello before she vented her frustration.

little trick can shorten your search time (and your annoyance level).

Addition Error

Many errors in adding are divisible by 10. For example, if the sum of three numbers is $475, you may have posted it as $465 or $485. There may be an addition error in the original posting or in the reconciliation itself. Check over your reconciliation first to see if you have an adding error there.

CASE STUDY

Becky felt much calmer when she finished her phone call with Vivian. Vivian had given her several strategies to troubleshoot the reconciliation problem.

Becky saw right away that her out-of-balance amount was divisible by nine, so she knew she was most likely looking for a transposition error. She carefully went through correcting entries again, searching for numbers that were turned around.

She found the problem a moment later. One of her entries should have been posted as $360, but she had posted it as $630. Once the correction was made, the reconciliation was completed in a few minutes.

Becky posted her notes on troubleshooting errors on her office wall in case she ran into this problem in the future.

Chapter Summary

- Reconciliation is the process of taking two numbers and explaining their differences.
- Transposition errors occur when two numbers are switched with each other. These errors are always divisible by nine.
- When a debit is posted as a credit, or vice versa, the error will be twice the original posting.
- Errors in addition are usually whole round numbers.

Chapter 18

When Your Books Are Already a Mess

In this chapter, you will learn:

- How to organize your documents to make bookkeeping easier
- How to inventory the mess and gather missing documents
- How to build a monthly financial statement package from the current chaos
- How to stay organized so that you can stay on top of your bookkeeping in the future
- When to hire a professional bookkeeper to record transactions in the future

Introduction

In a perfect world, as a small-business owner, you would set up your bookkeeping and accounting system before you begin operations. It gets you organized right out of the gate and sets you on the path of continuous record-keeping.

Real life, unfortunately, often intervenes and bookkeeping sometimes takes a back seat to other day-to-day business challenges. It can quickly build up and, the more daunting the pile, the less likely it will be tackled until finally there is no choice but to get it done. You may have notices from tax authorities inviting you to file returns or you may need financial statements to show your banker. Whatever the final impetus to get organized and get it done is, the bookkeeping won't account for itself. Where do you even start when you have shoe boxes — or maybe even refrigerator boxes — full of receipts, invoices, check stubs, flyers, product samples, and maybe even snacks or baby bottles?

By taking a step-by-step approach, you can whip your bookkeeping into shape and be able to produce accurate and timely financial statements in no time. The secret is organizing so that you know what you do and do not have. It's only then that you can fill in the gaps and gather the rest of the documents you need to do your transactional bookkeeping. The rest is easy!

Step 1: Organize the Mess

The first step is to separate out the important documents from non-accounting papers. It can be as simple as starting with two empty bankers' boxes, taking each item from your pile, and assessing its use. Accounting-related documents include invoices, receipts, purchase orders, check stubs, and deposit slips. These go in one box and everything else goes in the other, to be assessed further at a later time. Put the other box aside when you are done sorting and focus only on the accounting documents. This keeps the project manageable in size and time commitment.

Take all of the accounting documents and separate them into years if you are bookkeeping for more than one fiscal year. Starting with the first year's records, organize either by vendor, customer, expense type, or month. Most bookkeepers find that organizing by month results in quicker and more accurate input when looking at working on multiple months. It is easier to tie the transactions into the corresponding bank statements and to discover which documents you are missing.

Sorting the documents into their associated months can be accomplished through a set of file folders — one for each month. Label each folder clearly and order from oldest month to newest for each year. Once you have filed all of your piles into each month, take some time to search for any other accounting documents that you may have in other locations, like your inbox or in other files. The more you can locate upfront, the less time you will have to spend tracking them down later.

Step 2: Inventory the Documents

Once you have organized all of the accounting records that you can locate into their respective months, it is time to inventory what you actually have in order to be able to recognize what you are still missing.

At a minimum, each month should contain:

- The monthly bank statement
- Check stubs or a check register of all checks written in the month
- All invoices or cash register receipts issued in the month
- Copies of all deposit slips for the month
- All purchase receipts received during the month
- Any manual records of sales or expenses that you have maintained
- Receipts for business expenses paid by you personally

Set up a spreadsheet — either manual or computerized in a program such as Microsoft Excel — to check off which documents are complete and accounted for in each month and to highlight which paperwork you need to find. Duplicate bank statements can be ordered from the bank and duplicates of many receipts can be requested from vendors. If you do not have check stubs or copies of checks, you can order cancelled checks from many banks. In the future, ensure that you retain a check stub or a copy of each check written so that you can account for it in real time.

Receipts for purchases bought with personal funds should be separated from those purchased through the business account. Those purchased with company funds can be reconciled to the bank statements while those bought with your own money will generate an accounts payable or a credit to your equity account. Separating them will save time when entering them into the accounting system later.

Next, make a list of the missing documents that you will have to gather before you can begin bookkeeping. List them by document type so that, for example, you know which months' bank statements you need to order from the bank.

Step 3: Gather Missing Documents

At this point, you know what you have and what you need. Begin the search for missing documents in your office. Search through stacks of unopened mail on your desk, the bottom of your purse, and any other place you may have "temporarily"stored accounting documents.

Once you have determined that you have located everything in your possession, it's time to recreate what is still missing. Bank statements are among the easiest of documents to obtain copies of. If you have access to online banking, it can be as easy as printing the missing statements from the computer. If that is not possible or if you need the cancelled checks to go with them, you can order copies from your bank. Most banks charge for this service and it may take several days to continue your bookkeeping catch up while you wait for the statements to arrive.

For payment receipts for utilities, such as electricity or gas, begin by reviewing the company's website to see if you can obtain account information online. You can print off individual invoices or statements of your account on most online systems and this will save you time over ordering hard copies.

If, after your best efforts, you are unable to locate or recreate receipts for some expenses, you can use your bank statements (if the items were purchased with a debit card) or credit card statements (if your items were purchased with a credit card) as backup for the expense. While not as authoritative and useful if audited by tax authorities by virtue of purchase details and sales tax information being absent, it is better than having no source documents to back up the expense.

Step 4: Enter the Accounting Transactions

After gathering all of your source documents and sorting them into the correct periods, it's time to enter the transactions into your bookkeeping program. If you haven't yet chosen a bookkeeping program or system of recordkeeping, revisit Chapter 4 of this book to determine which bookkeeping system will work best for your particular situation.

In order to ensure that all of your transactions are recorded and that none are recorded twice, it is important to determine the entry starting point. If you haven't entered any transactions since your company opened its doors, simply begin at the beginning. If you have previously entered transactions, review them to assess how far along in the process you have progressed. Start with your first month of business and compare the transactions entered with the bank statement. If the transactions have all been entered, you can skip down to the next step and prepare a bank reconciliation for that month. In this way, you know that the month is complete. Complete as many bank reconciliations as possible for the months in which you have already entered transactions. In the first month with missing transactions, begin to account for your new receipts.

To help you remember whether you have entered a source document into your accounting system already, you can invest in an inked rubber stamp that says "Entered" and has a space to write in the date of entry. Stamp each document when entered to avoid duplicate entries that will later have to be reversed.

Step 5: Reconcile to the Bank Statements

Once all of your receipts, invoices, check stubs, and deposit slips have been accounted for in your bookkeeping system, reconcile them to the bank statements on a month-by-month basis. Detailed instructions about reconciliation appear in Chapters 16 and 17 of this book.

Ideally, you should have at least one source document for each bank statement entry. Certain automated payments such as car leases or equipment rentals may not have a monthly receipt. However, as these payments are likely to be the same amount each month, you can refer to the original agreements for details on the breakdown of these types of payments. You will also have to enter your bank fees and charges directly from the bank statements.

Reconciling your transactions to the bank statements ensures that you have entered all of your transactions that have affected your company's cash position. It is a final checkpoint to make sure the books are accurate. Print out a copy of each month's reconciliation after each is completed if using a computerized system.

Step 6: Create a Monthly Financial Statement Package

The final step in the process of catching up on your company's bookkeeping is to print off your monthly financial statements and keep them together with the original documents.

There are many ways to do this. An easy and organized method for small businesses is to use a 3-ring binder with monthly tab dividers. Use one binder for each fiscal year you are working on. A typical order of documents for each month would be:

- Balance sheet (as at the month's end)
- Monthly Income Statement (also known as a Profit & Loss Statement)
- Cash Flow Statement
- Bank Reconciliation
- Bank Statement
- Copies of invoices issued
- Copies of expense receipts
- Copies of check stubs
- Copies of deposit slips

Larger businesses may find it easier to use a binder for each month. Alternatively, you could set up each month in a file folder or even a bankers' box if you have that many source documents. Whichever method of organization you choose, it is important to set up a system that is easy to locate, search through, and retrieve from. The organization that you do now will also help you to keep on top of your bookkeeping going forward.

Step 7: Organize Your Bookkeeping for the Future

Once you have brought all of your company's bookkeeping to current, it's important to keep it that way. That might take a little self-analysis on your part. The first thing that you have to be honest with yourself about is why the bookkeeping got behind in the first place. Is it that you didn't have enough time with all of your other management responsibilities? Were you concerned that you didn't understand it well enough to attempt the bookkeeping? Do you simply dislike it? Knowing why your bookkeeping is behind will help you determine the best way to keep it up-to-date.

If the issue is time or interest, it is time to consider hiring a bookkeeper. If the thought of splurging on a professional bookkeeper horrifies both you and your pocketbook, consider what you are losing by not having your accounting up-to-date:

- Missing out on critical information about the recent financial direction of your company: This means that it will be almost impossible to steer your ship in a different direction before you hit the rocks.
- Late fees, interest on overdue balances, and other penalties because you didn't pay the company's bills on time or didn't file sales or property taxes by the due dates: Without having incoming bills and notices accounted for and filed in an organized way, it is difficult to know when bills are due and filings are required. It can often be more expensive paying interest and late fees than paying a professional bookkeeper to keep you up to date.
- Missing out on business opportunities: If your disorganization results in failing to realize that your newest product is not selling well but that there is renewed interest in an older product, you may miss the opportunity to adjust your sales and marketing plans to keep up with consumer trends. That can be a costly mistake — one that many businesses never recover from.
- Personal stress: Although not a financial consideration in the short term, it can be in the longer term. Stress caused by a less-than-desirable task being avoided can take its toll on your health over time. Knowing that it is being taken care of by a competent bookkeeper can relieve that stress and allow you to focus on other management considerations.

Chapter Summary

➡ No matter how long you have ignored your bookkeeping or what state it is in, it is never too late to take the reins and get control over your numbers. Not only will it help your tax reporting, it will help steer your business going forward. And it is one less thing to have to worry about as a small-business owner. Assess your own bookkeeping skills and your available time and make proactive decisions for getting your books caught up and keeping them that way.

ADVANCED ISSUES

Chapter 19

The Role of the External Accountant

In this chapter, you will learn —

- How to choose your accountant
- What your accountant can do for you
- What you should do yourself
- How to determine when you are outgrowing your accountant

In most major jurisdictions, there is no legal requirement to retain an accountant. You are allowed to handle all the tasks inherent in running a business, including bookkeeping, tax preparation, tax planning, financial statement preparation, and forecasting. However, there are many situations in which an accountant can help you navigate the murky waters of business management.

This chapter looks at how to choose an accountant, what your accountant does, and how to know when you have outgrown your accountant.

Choosing an Accountant

The word "accountant" really doesn't give you any information about the skills and training of the person you are looking to hire. The word itself is not regulated, as, for example, the word "lawyer" is. When you hear the word "lawyer" you understand immediately the training involved and the requirements for practice in the profession.

Not so with accountants. Anyone can call himself or herself an accountant and prepare your financial statements and tax returns. It's important to delve deep into the qualifications of the person you're about to hire.

Here are some important considerations to keep in mind when you are choosing your accountant:

- *Does he or she have a designation?* Designations such as Certified Public Accountant (CPA), Chartered

Accountant (CA), and Certified Management Accountant (CMA) are bestowed by organizations that require their members to have a certain level of knowledge and training as well as to adhere to a stringent professional code of conduct. Find out whether or not your accountant has these designations, then look up the website for that designation (websites are listed in Appendix B) and find out the level of qualification required. If you are searching for an accountant in your area, these organizations can direct you to local members.

- *How many clients does he or she have?* This point is important for two reasons. First, you want to make certain that you are not this person's first client (although, I suppose, someone has to be). You want an accountant with lots of experience with small businesses like yours. However, you want to make sure that your accountant is not going to be too busy to help you. Look at his or her office structure. Is there a live person at the front desk, or will you only ever get voicemail when you call? Are there other professional staff who can help you if the head accountant is busy? Can you ask them questions via email rather than play phone tag for days? It's important to ensure that your accountant will be there when you need him or her.
- *Is he or she keeping current with new software for small businesses?* This issue can be difficult to assess, but it is a concern. Some accountants (designated or not) do not assess new accounting software when it comes out and do not stay current with trends, therefore making it difficult for these accountants to recommend software to you. They would most likely simply recommend the software with which they are familiar because it's all they know.
- *Are his or her billing rates and policies clear?* Find out the firm's rates for different types of work. Some accountants will have set fees for work, and some will work on an hourly basis. If the firm bills on an hourly basis, make sure that your accountant will inform you of the costs accruing as the work progresses. There's nothing worse than getting a giant bill at the end that you weren't expecting.

And finally:

- *Do you like him or her?* You may have the best qualified accountant in the country but if you can't build a rapport with him or her, your working relationship will be very difficult. You will be more likely to take the advice of an accountant with whom you get along and whom you respect. Don't make the mistake of minimizing the importance of the relationship.

The Role of the Accountant

Your accountant can do many things for your business. The most common services accountants offer are the following:

- Bookkeeping support
- Setting up your financial transaction processing systems
- Assessing and refining your internal controls
- Compiling, reviewing, or auditing your financial statements

- Preparing your corporate income tax returns
- Helping you develop your growth and taxation strategies

How do you know what you want your accountant to do for you? When most businesses start up, the owners make the common mistake of thinking they can do everything themselves, because they feel they will lose control over what's happening if they don't. They are also trying to save a buck.

However, when it comes to hiring professional advisors — including accountants — scrimping will only hurt you in the long run. A regular half-hour meeting with your accountant can save you thousands of dollars and a lot of heartache and sleepless nights.

How often should you see your accountant? That varies for each business, but there are some critical junctures at which your accountant should be consulted.

Starting your business

Get your accountant involved from the beginning. Your accountant can advise you on the thousands of small details that every new business needs to attend to, from registering for sales tax to setting up your bookkeeping system, to planning owner remuneration. This initial meeting can save you an incredible amount of time and money.

Year end

Year end is the typical time most business owners see their accountants. Your accountant will make adjustments to your trial balance, prepare your financial statements, and calculate your corporate income tax returns.

At this meeting, discuss the upcoming year as well. Review the financials with your accountant and get him or her to explain any trends you see in your business but can't explain. Map out next year, looking at your budget and cash flow projection. Your accountant will give you tax planning advice that should include you as the owner of the business as well as the business itself. It's important to look at the taxation issues from a holistic perspective to make sure that the total tax is minimized and your compensation is maximized.

Employee evaluation and compensation

Your accountant can certainly help you with this task. It can be very difficult for a small-business owner to know how to evaluate company employees and how to remunerate them for their efforts.

Your accountant can help you design a performance evaluation system, including measurable targets, and can help set up a variable bonus or compensation system to reward employees for doing their jobs well. A compensation system motivates employees to do the things you need them to do to make the company profitable, which, ultimately, can be a great benefit to you.

Internal controls

Setting up appropriate financial controls in a small business is critical. You do not want to be left vulnerable to employee theft or asset mismanagement. Your accountant can help you structure employees' duties to minimize this risk. Your accountant can also make you aware of the warning signs of employee theft so that you can manage more effectively.

Management operating plan

Your budget and cash flow projections are a part of a larger financial management plan that you should maintain. I call it the management operating plan. Another book in the *Numbers 101* series, *Financial Management 101: Get a Grip on Your Business Numbers,* discusses this plan in detail. For now, it's enough to mention that your accountant can help you tailor the management operating plan to your needs and get it functioning for you.

Let's look now in more detail at the year-end process.

What the Accountant Needs from You at Year-End

Whew! You made it to the end of the year. You have accounted for all of the financial transactions in which your company has been engaged, you've reconciled the bank account and prepared or printed off a trial balance, and you're ready for the accountant to perform magic. What now?

There are several things that have to happen between the time you reconcile your last bank statement and the time your accountant hands you back the final financial statements. We'll look at both what you will need to do to "close off" your year and what your accountant does with the information you provide.

Every accountant will prefer to do things in a slightly different way at year end, but here are the general things you should have ready:

- **Trial balance:** This document is the one your accountant will use to prepare the financial statements.
- **General journal detail:** Your accountant may need to see how you have prepared some of your transactions.
- **Bank reconciliation:** Your accountant will want to make sure you did it correctly.
- **Bank statements:** Have at least the year-end statement available so your accountant can compare it to your bank reconciliation.
- **Check stubs:** To make sure that you have recorded all of the outstanding checks, your accountant will need to see the check stubs.
- **Accounts receivable and payable listings:** The accountant will want to see an aged listing of your receivables and payables.
- **Government remittance forms and statements of account:** The accountant may want to reconcile your books to what the government thinks you owe.
- **Corporate notice of assessment from last year:** The accountant will check that the tax returns your company filed were assessed by the government and not changed.

If your accountant is reviewing or auditing your financial statements rather than just preparing them, he or she may want many more documents and, at year-end, will provide you with a list of these.

The Process of Creating Financial Statements

Your trial balance and other source documents are now safe in the hands of your accountant. What does he or she actually do with them? You give your accountant papers, and he or she gives you papers back. Are they just the same as what you provided in the first place? What the heck is your accountant doing that's costing you so much money?

The first thing that your accountant does is prepare the financial statements. These statements may look much like the balance sheet and income statement that you print off from your software package, but there will be some differences.

It's the accountant's job to prepare the financial statements on an accrual basis, because that is what GAAP tells the accountant to do. The accountant will make adjusting journal entries to your statements based on what your bookkeeping has captured or missed. Here are some of the common adjusting entries:

- **Capital asset depreciation:** It is common to leave this entry for the accountant to calculate and post.
- **Accrued liabilities:** The obvious one is the estimated accounting fee. It's a cost that belongs in the year to which it relates, so the accountant will expense it and set up the liability.
- **Outstanding checks:** If you have been working on a cash basis throughout the year, the accountant will have to set up those checks that were written but not cleared through the bank by the end of the year.
- **Allowance for Doubtful Accounts (AFDA):** Your accountant may ask you if there are any receivables that you believe are uncollectible and will set up an allowance and an expense for these.
- **Prepaid expenses:** Some of your supplier payments may be for things that relate to next year. If you have not adjusted for the prepaid portion, your accountant will.

Once the accountant has posted all of the adjusting journal entries, he or she will prepare a balance sheet, income statement, cash flow statement, and notes to those statements on his or her letterhead. At the beginning of the set of financials, your accountant will write a standard report on the extent of what he or she did. If the statements have simply been prepared (as opposed to reviewed or audited), the report will look something like this:

NOTICE TO READER

I have compiled the balance sheet of Small Company Inc. as at 31 December 2003 and the statements of income, retained earnings, and cash flows for the year then ended from information provided by management. I have not audited, reviewed, or otherwise attempted to verify the accuracy or completeness of such information. Readers are cautioned that these statements may not be appropriate for their purposes.

Your accountant will then sign the bottom of the report. This report is focused on the readers of your financial statements to help them understand the nature and extent of the work that was done on them. It forms an integral part of the financial statement package and should be left in when you provide your statements to banks or other financial statement users.

Corporate Income Tax Returns

Once the financial statements have been prepared, the corporate income tax returns need to be prepared for all levels of government that require them.

Your accountant will take the income figures from the financial statements he or she has just prepared and will adjust them for any necessary differences between book and tax. For example, a portion of the meals and entertainment expense must be added back into income for tax purposes, as it is not 100 percent deductible.

Once the balances for income taxes owing are calculated, the accountant must make an entry in the financial statements to accrue this liability. Then, both the financials and the tax returns are finalized and presented to you for signing.

Posting the Adjusting Journal Entries

Now that you have the financials and tax returns back from your accountant, it is time to start closing off the year. The first step in this process is to post the accountant's adjusting entries to your bookkeeping system. This action keeps your records in step with the final financial statements.

The accountant will have given you a listing of the journal entries he or she had to make as a result of the preparation of the statements. You will post them to your journal as of the last day of the year. Be careful to post them to the appropriate year. If you are on a manual system, just leave enough room in the old journal to post the entries. You will have to wait until you get the entries back from the accountant before you record the new year's opening balances; otherwise, some will be incorrect.

If you are on a computerized system, you will need to have a good understanding of how the program handles posting to the new year. In the current versions of most software, you are allowed to continue your day-to-day posting in the new year without closing off the old year. If your software does not have that capability, you will have to hold off on any bookkeeping for the new year until you have posted the adjusting entries for the old year and have rolled forward. This situation could leave you with a backlog of a month or two of bookkeeping. It's especially impractical if you use your bookkeeping system to print invoices and checks.

Once the entries have been posted, print off a balance sheet and income statement for the prior year. Double check that you have the same figures in your journals as are in the final financial statements, especially the retained earnings. If you roll the year forward and there are discrepancies, they will be a hassle to fix.

When all the balances match, it's time to close off the year and roll forward.

Rolling Forward the Year

The process of close off and roll forward simply clears out your income statement accounts so that you can start fresh for the new year. Your balance sheet accounts carry forward, but the income and expense accounts roll up into retained earnings.

If you are on a manual system, your closing entry will debit your revenue accounts and credit your expense accounts to bring them to zero. The difference is debited or credited (as the case may be) to retained earnings.

If you are on a computerized system, there will be a close-off procedure to perform as well. It's very important, however, to save a backup copy of the final figures from the prior year. Keep this backup separate from your daily backups so that you know that it is the final one. Once you have done that, and you have read the system documentation for the roll-forward procedure, you can perform that task.

Now you are ready to start your new year!

How Do You Know When You're Outgrowing Your Accountant?

Every accounting firm has a different focus. Some strictly do personal income tax. Others focus on the needs of small-business owners. Still others specialize in management consulting to large corporations. Even within these categories, there are differences in firms.

For example, some smaller accounting firms deal only with basic small-business issues. They may be able to prepare simple financial statements and corporate income tax returns, but may be unable to answer your questions about employee compensation or buy/sell agreements.

Here are some things to consider when deciding if your company is growing too complex for your accountant:

- *Does your accountant return your phone calls promptly when you have a complex issue to discuss?* If not, this could be a sign that he or she is not comfortable giving counsel on that particular issue.
- *Does your accountant have access to expert help for issues that are outside of his or her area of knowledge?* For example, some accounting firms have arrangements with tax or export specialists to assist their clients with these types of issues. If yours does not, you will have to consider what will happen if you face these issues.
- *Is your accountant frequently making errors in your statements or forgetting business transactions that you had previously discussed with him or her?* This could be a signal that your accountant is either too busy or isn't focusing on your business needs — two situations that spell risk for you.

At the end of every year, assess the performance of your accountant (as well as your other business advisors) to ensure that he or she is still a good fit for your business. If you feel that any of the above situations are occurring, sit down with your accountant and discuss them candidly. If you find the answers are insufficient to address your concerns, it's time to find another accountant.

Chapter Summary

- When choosing your accountant, look for attributes like designation, experience, and rapport.
- Choose your accountant when you first start in business, not after you are already in a mess.
- At the end of every year, your accountant takes your ledgers, makes adjusting year-end entries, and uses that information to produce the final financial statements and the income tax returns.
- Reassess your choice of accountants yearly and recognize when your business has outgrown your accountant.

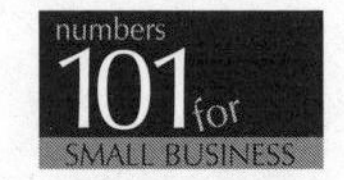

Chapter 20

Budgeting: Planning for the Future

In this chapter, you will learn —

- Why budgeting is important
- Structuring the budget
- How to project forward from your historical performance
- How to keep the budget up-to-date

Yuck! Budgeting. You knew we'd get here. There's no avoiding it. Budgeting (no matter what you think of it) is a critical part of your company's life. Without a plan, your business will drift.

Another book in the *Numbers 101* series, *Financial Management 101: Get a Grip on Your Business Numbers* looks at the entire planning process in more depth. The goal of this chapter, however, is to lay the foundation of that process: to look at what makes up the budget, how to set one up, and how to monitor and update it. Who knows? By the end of this chapter, it may just be fun!

But How Do I Know What's Going to Happen in the Future?

I hear this complaint a lot. Small business owners, already mired in the day-to-day operations of their companies, throw up their hands when told that they should maintain a budget. "But who knows what my sales are going to be? Insurance is on the rise, and I have no idea by how much. How can I possibly plan 12 months into the future?"

The fact is, if you don't know where you're going, you won't know how to get there. A budget gives you a road map. You may end up on a different road, but at least you've created the path.

A budget also gives you a dose of reality. If, for example, you want to move into new premises that will cost you an extra $20,000 in operating expenses per year, and you put that into your budget, you may find that you need to sell an extra 9,500 units of product to cover the increase in the expense. If your current sales structure cannot support an extra 9,500 units, you have big problems. It's better to find out before you move to the new location.

It's important to understand the difference between a budget and a cash-flow projection. Budgets generally encompass only revenues and expense items, whereas cash flows track all cash inflows and outflows: income, investments, loans, and repayments. A budget will be prepared on an accrual basis just as the income statement is, whereas the cash-flow projection will be on a cash basis. (See Chapter 21 for more information on cash-flow projections.)

Setting up the 12-Month Budget

The steps to setting up a 12-month budget are straightforward:

1. *Prepare (or print off) an income statement for the past 12 months.* It doesn't matter at what point in your fiscal year you begin this process. You will always be looking 12 months in the past and 12 months in the future. Any 12-month window will encompass a full operating cycle, regardless of the month with which you begin. Evaluate the revenue and expense categories. Do they give you enough information about your cost structure? For example, if you have an expense line called advertising and promotion, does that tell you enough about where you are spending your advertising dollars, or would a finer breakdown be helpful? You might make sub-categories of advertising and promotion, such as print ads, radio spots, mailings, or brochure printing. In some cases, further breakdown won't give you any more information than you already have.

   If you want to adjust your categories, do it now. If you are breaking out pieces of categories, make sure that the past 12 months are broken out the same way. Then you can compare the past 12 months to future periods.

2. *Once your categories are structured the way you want to see them, prepare a monthly comparative income statement for the past 12 months.* If you are working manually, doing so may take some time, but if you are on a computerized system, the monthly comparative income statement should be one of the available reports. You want to look over the last 12 months to get a better understanding of historical performance, to see the revenue and expense trends in the business. For example, it may surprise you to find out that your office supplies account fluctuates in almost perfect lockstep with your revenues. You may not notice this relationship until you perform this review. Would the behavior of your expenses be good information to have when you prepare your 12-month budget? Of course it would!

   Look at your monthly revenues. Do they stay relatively the same from month to month? Do they show an upward trend? Or are they more cyclical, spiking during your peak sales season and tapering off after that? Knowing your revenue trends helps you predict what the revenues will be next year.

3. *Set up the budget spreadsheet if you are working manually.* Most computer software programs allow you to input budget numbers so that you can always compare actual to budget performance. Use the same categories that you have developed for the income statement. You will need columns for each of the next 12 months and a total column at the end. In your rows, make total lines for revenues, expenses, and net income, much like you have on your income statement.

   Worksheet 3 is a blank budget template that you are welcome to photocopy and use.

Aren't I Just Making up Fake Numbers?

You may feel strange the first few times you work on your budget. You may feel as if you could make up anything. It's in the future. Anything's possible, right?

Not exactly. The more thoroughly you have examined your historical performance, the more accuracy you will have in projecting the future. For example, if you have been in business for four years and your company is still growing, most likely your revenues will be no lower than last year's total. Now you have a floor for your projection. If your revenues appear to increase by a sedate 5 percent per year, chances are, barring any major changes to your operations, they will increase by 5 percent next year. Simply multiply last year's revenues by 1.05, and you will have your projected revenues.

On the expense side, you should now have a good handle on which expenses stay the same and which ones increase with changes in revenues (or other costs). Once you have projected the revenue, you can project the same percentage increase in those costs (if they move in tandem).

Fill in the rest of the expense items. Once you have completed the preliminary budget, check it one more time against the last 12 months. Does it still look reasonable? If not, rework it until you're comfortable that it makes sense.

Changes to the Company's Operations

Now that you are comfortable that the budget for the next 12 months makes sense in comparison with the last 12, you need to review your management operating plan. We look at how to put together a management operating plan in the second book in this series, but for now, just think of it as your plans for your business. It maps out the changes you want to make: change in premises, increase in sales efforts, more radio ads, etc. Your management operating plan also projects the financial impact these changes will likely have on your business.

The next step is to review the preliminary budget and adjust it for the changes that you know will happen in the next 12 months (called fine-tuning). Are you renting new warehouse space next July? Make sure the budget reflects the extra lease payments. Are you hiring a new salesperson? Make sure both the salary and the projected increase in revenue are in the budget.

By now, you will have your road map for the next year. The budget will become part of your cash-flow projections, but when compared to your actual performance, can provide you with a wealth of information.

Worksheet 3
BUDGET TEMPLATE

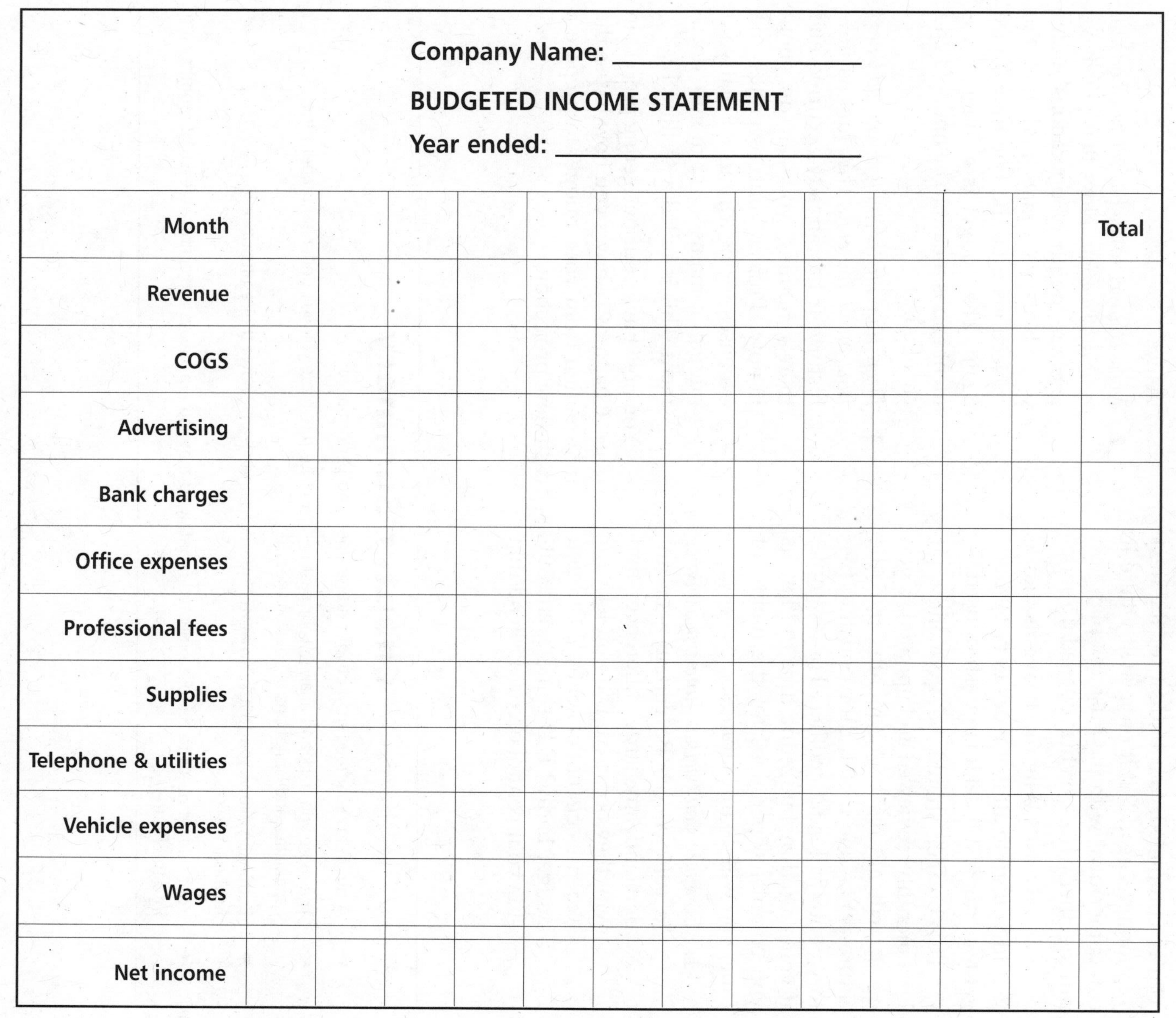

Company Name: ______________

BUDGETED INCOME STATEMENT

Year ended: ______________

Month													Total
Revenue													
COGS													
Advertising													
Bank charges													
Office expenses													
Professional fees													
Supplies													
Telephone & utilities													
Vehicle expenses													
Wages													
Net income													

Rolling, Rolling, Rolling, Keep That Budget Rolling

You've completed your budget for the next 12 months. Great! Put it on a shelf where it can gather dust with the business plan you put together when you first opened up shop.

Not so fast! Why in heaven's name would you go to all that work to put a budget together just to let it languish unused?

The budget should be frequently (at least monthly) reviewed and updated as you go. It will always be 12 months into the future, so as one month drops off into history, you will add another. For example, if you started by budgeting June to May, as you complete operations for the month of June, you will do three things:

1. *Compare your actual June performance to your budget.* Be certain you understand any large differences and why they occurred. Did you let your expenses get out of control? Did you budget badly? Did some event outside your control occur? Pretend that you have to explain the results to a board of directors. How would you characterize your company's performance?
2. *Make changes to the budget based on any new information.* Now that you have another month of operations under your belt, you may find that the projections must be fine tuned once again. The budget is a living document and is meant to be updated and changed.
3. *Drop June off the budget and add next June on at the end.* This June is now history. It has already occurred and there's nothing you can do about it now. Project your revenues and expenses for next June, so that your budget remains a 12-month document. This is called a "rolling 12."

You now have your budgeting process in place. Chapter 21 shows you how to use the information from your budget to prepare a cash-flow projection.

Chapter Summary

- A budget is your road map of your future operating performance.
- The more you track and analyze your past performance, the more you will understand about the capabilities and limitations of your business.
- Budgeting allows you to ask "what if?" questions and clearly shows the results of various financial choices.
- Your budget needs to be rolled forward monthly so that you are always projecting at least 12 months into the future.

Chapter 21

Monitoring Cash Flow: How Not to Run out of Money

In this chapter, you will learn —

- How to recognize when you're going to hit the money wall
- Methods of stretching your cash
- How and when to barter
- How to avoid the crunch in the future

What Is Cash Flow?

Cash flow is simply the difference between the money coming in to a business from all sources and the money going out of the business. If there's more money coming in than going out, it's called a surplus. If there is more going out than coming in, it's called a deficit.

What's the Difference between Cash Flow and Net Income?

There are many things that affect the cash flow of a business that are not directly related to its income statement. For example, if you buy a new company truck, the cash outlay affects your cash flow (because money went out), but the truck will be set up as a capital asset on the balance sheet and therefore won't appear on the income statement. It will start to hit the income statement in small pieces when you depreciate it.

Cash flow represents real time movement of cash, whereas the income statement shows the results of operations by using the accrual method (more on this later). An example of this is that sales will show up on an income statement as soon as they occur, even if you haven't received the money yet. This sale won't impact the cash flow of the business until it is collected. The length of time it takes to collect the money from that sale can help or hurt the cash-flow position of the business.

CASE STUDY

Joe sat down at the kitchen table with Becky and looked through the financial statements again. He couldn't understand why his income statement said he made $43,000 so far this year, but his bank account had no money in it.

The bank loan payment was coming due in four days, and Becky had several calls a day from their suppliers, wanting to be paid for overdue invoices. The largest invoice was $18,000 for plumbing parts that Joe had bought to have on hand for future jobs.

Every time Joe got some money from a customer, it went right out the door again. Becky called their customers frequently to bring in some of their receivables, but the problem that was plaguing Joe and Becky also seemed to be affecting their customers: not enough money to pay their bills.

Joe had tried talking to his bank manager about an additional short-term loan. The bank manager had at least appeared to solemnly consider it, but in the end, he turned Joe down, explaining that Joe's current cash flow problems made the bank nervous about his future prospects and his ability to pay back the loan.

Joe and Becky were both frustrated. It seemed as if the bank lent only to businesses that didn't need the money. Joe picked up the phone and called his accountant for advice.

How Do I Know When My Business Is Going to Run out of Money?

You should develop a projected cash flow statement for the business at the same time you prepare the budget (discussed in Chapter 19). Some of the same information is used in both the budget and cash flow statements, but there are some adjustments necessary. A detailed discussion of the cash flow projection can be found in another book in the *Numbers 101 for Small Business* series, *Financial Management 101: Get a Grip on Your Business Numbers.* Also, Microsoft Excel templates are available on my website, www.numbers101.com.

Your cash flow statement will show you month-by-month what both your net cash in and out and your running total of cash will be. When your cumulative cash balance is negative, the deficit must be covered by some means; for example, by a line of credit.

This statement will also show you your business cycle, which is really important information to have. There will be times during the year when the business is busier than usual. The corresponding peaks of incoming cash, however, will lag behind your business peak times by 30 to 90 days, depending on how tight your accounts receivable policies are. You should ensure that the money collected from your peak business months will cover your expenses for the rest of the year.

Building Your Company's War Chest

Preserving your company's cash is more important than ever. Banks across North America are tightening up their lending criteria for small businesses, and funds are becoming scarce. Successful businesses must rally their own resources to ensure that there is enough money to carry them through the hard times.

Once you have completed the first step of developing your projected cash flow (don't forget to include the money you want to pay yourself!), you can start planning.

For example, let's say you found yourself with an extra $27,000 in your bank account at the end of August. Great. You may decide to use the money to buy new equipment, or you may simply want to draw out the surplus. However, by the end of December, you may find you need $24,500 of that $27,000 to cover expenses. Without a solid understanding of cash flow, you might use up your surplus, not realizing that you will need it for operating expenses months down the road.

One way to keep the surplus safe until you need it is to set up a separate bank account for it. That way, you will have to make a conscious decision to draw on the funds, and it won't just "disappear." You can keep this money invested in a liquid and short-term investment such as a money-market fund, or you can seek out one of the higher-interest savings accounts offered by some banks and trust companies. Always keep the surplus working for you, but make sure you can access it when you need it.

How Can I Stretch My Company's Cash Further?

There are many ways to make sure that you are using your company's resources in the most efficient way possible. Ask yourself the following questions regarding your accounts receivable, accounts payable, inventory, and long-term debt:

Accounts Receivable

- What is my company's receivables policy? (e.g., due in 30 days)
- What is my actual average collection time on my receivables?
- Is there any penalty for my customers for paying late?
- Is there any incentive for them to pay early?
- Are my receivable and collection policies clear to my customers?
- Do I follow up regularly with overdue accounts?
- Do I make it easy or difficult for my customers to pay?

Many small businesses are astonished to find that their actual collection time bears no relation to their official accounts receivable policies. Not collecting receivables on time is one of the biggest drags on cash flow for a business. Make it easy for your customers to pay you by taking the following steps:

- Offer a discount for early payment.
- Charge interest on overdue accounts.
- Produce monthly receivable statements for your customers and follow up on them.
- Accept as many forms of payment as you can: cash, check, debit cards, and credit cards. The increase in the speed of payment will more than offset the costs of accepting credit and debit cards. You may also attract new customers.

Accounts Payable

- Do I have a good tracking system for my payables?

- Am I chronically paying suppliers late and having to pay penalties?
- Am I paying too early and not taking advantage of my suppliers' credit terms?
- Do I know how much money I will have to put aside at any given time to pay my debts?

Having a good tracking system is critical for cash management. It allows you to know your upcoming cash requirements at any point in time. Take full advantage of your suppliers' credit terms but be certain that you're not getting zinged with late charges and interest.

Inventory

- How long does it take me to sell my inventory?
- Do I buy inventory items that become obsolete or unsaleable before I can sell them?
- How long does it take between ordering and receiving an inventory item?

Keeping and warehousing inventory can be very expensive, especially when market conditions are continually changing and you risk having a warehouse full of obsolete product. Keep inventory levels to a minimum and order as you need product. Be careful, however, that you are not inconveniencing your customers by making them wait while you order product.

Long-Term Debt

- Am I able to renegotiate my bank loans if I need to in order to reduce cash outflows?
- Am I getting the best interest rate possible?

At least once a year, sit down and analyze your borrowing needs. Ensure that you are getting the best interest rate and that your bank is looking after all your needs. There will always be other banks that want your business. It pays to shop around! Another book in this series, *Financial Management 101,* takes an in-depth look at financing.

Barter: A Small-Business Owner's Secret Weapon

The concept of bartering goods and services is not a new one. It was practiced for thousands of years before hard currency took over as the basic facilitator of trade. But how can barter help a small business today?

If your business is cash-strapped, you can help preserve your war chest by "purchasing" a needed good or service without using money. In exchange for the good or service you have received, you will offer your products or services as "payment."

How can you find people with whom you can barter? Many cities have organized barter networks, through which members provide their goods and services to other members of the network for "barter dollars." They can then purchase goods and services from other network members with their accounts.

When using a barter network, you don't have to exchange with each individual member from whom you want to purchase. For example, if you want to use the graphic design services of Kelly, but she doesn't need your plumbing services, she does the work for you anyway and receives barter dollars that she can spend elsewhere on the network.

If there isn't a barter network in your community, there will still be many small

CASE STUDY

Joe felt much better after his planning session with his accountant. They had discussed Joe's accounts receivables, payables, and inventory. Together, they developed the following plan:

Becky will formalize the billing and accounts receivable processes. All bills will be produced and mailed the day after the service has been provided. Joe will offer a 5 percent discount if the invoice is paid in full within 7 days of the invoice date, and the bill is otherwise due in 30 days. Joe will charge interest on overdue bills at 2 percent per month. Becky will call customers on day 30 and (if necessary) day 45 and will send statements out on the first of every month. On day 60, she will call customers to tell them that the invoice needs to be paid in 7 days or she will turn the account over to a collection agency. All of their new billing terms will be printed on their invoices.

- Joe will stop buying plumbing supplies to put in inventory. His major supplier can ship parts in 24 hours, so Joe doesn't need to hold back a supply. He also found out that he could return the $18,000 in parts he already purchased for a full refund.
- Becky will monitor the accounts payable more closely, especially the due dates. She will mail payments four business days before the due date to ensure that the payment reaches the supplier on time.
- Joe will approach the bank again after the busy summer and fall season. His financial statements will look better, and his chances for obtaining financing will be improved. He will try to negotiate a line of credit as a buffer for his slow seasons.

business groups whose members can unofficially make arrangements with each other to barter wares.

There are some important dos and don'ts for bartering:

- In most countries, you must claim barter income for income and retail tax purposes. Likewise, you may claim deductions for barter business expenses. Check with your accountant for the laws in your jurisdiction.
- Purchase only barter items that you need for your business. Treat barter dollars as you would real money and don't overspend.
- Make sure that you are comfortable with the quality of the services provided by the network members you deal with. You should assess the quality just as you would if you were paying cash for the item.
- If you are engaged in an informal barter arrangement, draw up a written agreement as to the amounts agreed upon and the time frame for completion. Ensure that both parties have the same understanding of the nature of the arrangement.

Accounting for barter transactions

If you are part of an organized barter exchange, you will receive barter-dollar statements that will look much like bank statements. The only difference in the accounting is that you will set up a separate asset account to account for the barter dollars.

When you receive or pay barter dollars, you will debit or credit that account. You will also reconcile it just as you would a regular bank account.

If you're not part of an organized exchange, the accounting gets a little more difficult. You must first decide the value of the transaction. For example, if you have a pool maintenance company and you provide pool cleaning services to your neighbor in exchange for landscaping services for your office building, the value of the transaction is the value of the service provided, or, if that can't be determined, the value of the service received. In this example, let's say that you normally charge $125 for the pool cleaning (ignore taxes for now). That would be the value of the transaction. You would make the following entry in your books:

DR	**Landscaping expense**	**$125.00**	
CR	**Revenue**		**$125.00**

If the service provided to you is for personal purposes, like landscaping at your home, you would debit the shareholder loan account (or the owner's equity account in the case of an unincorporated business) instead.

The Future: How to Avoid the Cash Crunch before It Hits

There are no magic tricks for making sure that you don't hit the wall in the future. You must constantly monitor your business results as well as both your budget and your cash flow. In larger businesses, the chief financial officer performs these tasks, but if you don't have the budget for a CFO, the CFO's duties will become your responsibility as an owner/manager. Block off time in your day planner (What? You don't have a day planner? Get one!) to review your financial results once a month. Your business will prosper because of it!

A more in-depth discussion of the planning process appears in another book in the *Numbers 101 for Small Business* series, *Financial Management 101: Get a Grip on Your Business Numbers.*

Chapter Summary

- Cash flow and net income are different things. Cash flow is the difference between the money coming into a business and the money going out of it.
- You should develop a projected cash flow statement for your business to show in which months you can expect to have deficits to finance and in which months you can expect surpluses to sock away in your war chest.
- Review your accounts receivable, accounts payable, and inventory policies to make sure that you are using your company's resources efficiently.
- Bartering goods and services can be a great way to preserve money.

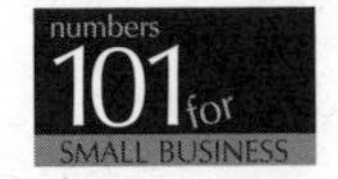

Chapter 22

A Brief Look at Foreign Currency

In this chapter, you will learn —

- How to account for foreign currency bank accounts
- How to post foreign currency transactions
- Revaluation of your foreign currency holdings at year end
- Mitigation of foreign exchange risks

Many small businesses have to deal with foreign currencies at some point. You may purchase goods from a foreign supplier or sell to a foreign purchaser. You may go on a business trip abroad and have expenses to document.

Foreign currency is an area that is often handled poorly by small-business bookkeepers. This chapter will touch on the major issues and will show you how to account for the most common types of foreign currency transactions.

Occasional Foreign Currency Transactions

If your business has only the occasional foreign currency transaction, you probably do not maintain a bank account in that currency. For example, say you are located in Canada and you bought a one-time shipment of goods from a US vendor. You would probably direct your Canadian bank to prepare a US dollar bank draft and to take the equivalent Canadian dollars out of your bank account.

In this situation, you need to track the original US dollar amount of the purchase until you pay it. Problems arise when the relative values of the US and Canadian dollars change during this period.

Let's look at an example: You have purchased $1,000 USD worth of goods from a supplier in North Carolina. You will pay them in 30 days. The US dollar exchange rate is 1.529 on the date of purchase. You need to record the transaction in Canadian dollars, as that is the currency in which you are reporting. When you take possession of the goods, you will make the following entry:

DR	**Inventory**	**$1,529.00**	
CR	**US $ accounts payable**		**$1,000.00**
CR	**Exchange on US $ payables**		**529.00**

The exchange account is a liability account, just like the rest of the payables. Separating the US dollar payable from the exchange allows you always to be able to track the original billing amount in the US dollar accounts payable account.

The other side of the entry (in this case, inventory, but in other cases, it could be an expense account) records the full value of the transaction on the date of purchase. Purchases and sales are recorded at historical rates, so you will never revalue this part of the entry.

Thirty days later, you pay your supplier. The US dollar exchange rate is now 1.536, so you know that the bank will withdraw $1,536 to cover the $1,000 USD draft. However, there's only $1,529 in accounts payable. How do you account for the difference?

The difference represents the loss on the transaction. Had you settled the bill on the day you purchased the goods, you would have had to pay only $1,529. But because you waited 30 days, the exchange rate changed and now you must pay more. The entry to record the payment is —

DR	**Accounts payable**	**$1,529.00**	
DR	**Exchange loss (expense)**	**7.00**	
CR	**Cash**		**$1,536.00**

You do not have to record the us portion of the cash separately, as the bank is doing the conversion directly. When you receive your bank statement, it will show only the $1,536. This amount will match your entry.

The Foreign Currency Bank Account

If you have regular foreign currency transactions, you most likely have a bank account denominated in that currency. Let's have a look at how that works, using the information in the above example.

The entry to record the purchase and accounts payable is the same. The only difference happens when you record the payment. If you maintain a separate US dollar bank account, the transactions are recorded in US dollars with the exchange recorded in a separate cash account. To pay your supplier, you will write a check for $1,000 USD. The accounting entry would look like this:

DR	**US Accounts payable**	**$1,000.00**	
DR	**Exchange on US $ payables**	**529.00**	
CR	**US $ cash**		**$1,000.00**
CR	**Exchange on US $ cash**		**536.00**
DR	**Exchange loss**	**7.00**	

This entry looks a bit complex, but break it down into what it tells you. The account is no longer payable, so you need to clear out the original payable amount (which was $1,000 in the US dollar payable account and $529 in the exchange on US dollar payable account). You cut a check for $1,000 USD, so the US bank account needs to reflect this. The $1,000 is now worth an additional $536, so this amount must be credited to the total bank amount. There was a loss of $7 on holding the payable, which gets expensed on the income statement.

Revaluation at Year End

In most countries, GAAP requires that you carry your foreign currency cash and claims on cash (receivables and payables) at the current exchange rate at the end of every period. For example, let's say your business is located in the US, and the only foreign currency transaction into which you entered during the year was a sale to a Canadian customer in Canadian dollars (and you have a Canadian dollar bank account). The sale is for $1,500 CAD, and the customer has paid you. The exchange rate on that day was 0.654. Your bank account would be stated in your books as —

CAD $ bank	**$1,500.00**
Exchange on CAD $ bank	**(518.97)**

The sum of these two cash accounts represents the US dollar equivalent of that Canadian cash ($981.03).

At your year end, the exchange rate is now 0.672. Your Canadian cash is now worth $1,008. We need to make an entry to reflect the increase in value. The entry looks like this:

DR	**Exchange on CAD $ bank**	**$26.97**	
CR	**Exchange gain (income)**		**$26.97**

The cash is now valued at its year end value on the statements. You would perform this same adjustment to the foreign currency receivables and payables.

Reconciling the Foreign Currency Bank Account

The reconciliation process for foreign currency bank accounts is really not that different from the process for domestic accounts. The only difference is that you will reconcile the account in the foreign currency.

For example, if you are a Canadian company with a pounds sterling bank account, the bank statement will show in pounds sterling. You will have an account in your ledger called "Pounds sterling bank" or something similar. Only pounds will be in this account. All of the exchange amounts to value it in Canadian dollars will be in another cash account called "Exchange on pounds sterling account" or something similar. You do not need to reconcile this account, because you will be adjusting it to actual at the end of every period.

Foreign Currency Risk

Every time you hold foreign currency or claims to foreign currency (receivables and payables) you incur foreign currency risk. Quite simply, it's the risk that exchange rates will change, which they invariably do.

If you are a Canadian company and a significant portion of your revenues comes from the US, but all your payables are paid to Canadian companies, you will win when the US dollar exchange rate goes up but will lose when it goes down. The reverse is true if you purchase from the US but sell in Canada. If you purchase and sell in US dollars, there is very little risk because you will gain on one side and lose on the other.

If you have significant dollars tied up in foreign currency transactions, you may want to find more formal ways to minimize the risks. One way to do that is through hedging contracts.

Hedging contracts allow you to purchase or sell foreign currencies at a specific time for a specific price.

Here's how they work: You are a US company selling product to Australia. You will be receiving Australian dollars in 60 days for a large shipment of goods. You are very concerned about the exchange rate trend lately, and you are worried that the Australian dollar will be worth less by the time you receive the payment. If so, you will get less value for the goods you shipped.

A hedging contract allows you to fix the price of the sale. Let's say that the Australian dollar is worth 0.617 to the US dollar. You have sold $10,000 AUD worth of product to a customer in Brisbane. At the date of sale, its value is $6,170 USD. You set up your receivable for this amount. You are concerned that the Australian exchange rate will drop to 0.597 in 30 days, which is when you expect to receive payment. As a result, you would get only $5,970 worth of value. You would lose $200 USD just for holding the receivable.

You would buy a foreign currency contract stipulating that you sell $10,000 AUD for 0.612 in 30 days. You would pay a premium to do this. Let's assume the premium costs you $30 USD. Here's what your cash flows look like, assuming the Australian dollar does go down to 0.597:

1. You pay a premium of $30 USD for the hedging contract.
2. You receive the equivalent of $5,970 in 30 days from the customer. Therefore, you have an exchange loss on the sale of $200 USD.
3. You take the $10,000 AUD that you received from your customer and sell it per the contract at 0.612. You gain $150 on the transaction because you are selling something for the equivalent of $6,120 that's worth only $5,970 in the open market.

Looking at all these things together, you have lost $80 ($150 – $200 – $30). Remember that had you not entered into the contract, you would have lost $200. Hedging foreign currency positions is a useful strategy that businesses of all sizes can use to reduce the risk of importing and exporting.

Chapter Summary

- You have a currency gain or loss when you settle a foreign-denominated transaction at a different exchange rate than the one at which the original transaction took place.
- Foreign currency bank accounts are reconciled in their native dollars.
- In most countries, foreign currency bank, accounts receivable, and accounts payable balances must be revalued at the period-end exchange rate in order to comply with GAAP.
- Foreign currency risk arises when your cash inflows are in one currency and your outflows are in another.

Chapter 23

Tax Planning

In this chapter, you will learn —

- The concept of tax integration
- How to maximize income and minimize taxes
- How to plan your personal revenue streams

Granted, tax is not one of the top ten most fun things to talk about on anyone's list. However, tax planning is an area that you and your accountant should work on together. The way in which your profits are taxed affects how much money you get to keep. This chapter gives you an overview of some of the strategies and issues to keep in mind. It's always important to be familiar with the tax legislation in your jurisdiction before you embark on any strategy. The last thing you want is the nasty surprise of a big tax bill.

Minimizing Tax versus Avoiding Tax

Nobody likes paying tax (not even me!), but without taxation, the government wouldn't have the money it needs to provide all the programs and services that it does. Tax, therefore, is a necessary evil.

As a taxpayer, personally and corporately, you are fully entitled to plan your affairs so as to minimize the tax you pay. You can choose the best way to pay yourself, deduct all of the expenses that are legitimately for business purposes, and set up the corporate structure that best minimizes the tax bill.

However, there is another category of "tax planning" called tax avoidance, and it is illegal. You are engaging in tax avoidance when you hide income, deduct fictitious expenses or expenses that are not related to the business, and when you don't declare all your sources of income. There are a few good reasons to stay away from this kind of "planning":

1. *It's illegal:* Most jurisdictions have an anti-avoidance rule. If you are caught, you could face significant fines and penalties and could go to jail. (It's really hard to run a small business from jail.)
2. *It's a waste of time:* It falls into the category of "Oh, what a tangled web we weave, when first we practice to deceive." Hiding income and faking expenses takes time. If, instead, you spent that time on building your business and getting more money in the door (even if it is taxed), you would be far better off in the long run.
3. *Eventually, it will make you lose sleep:* Most taxation authorities can go back in time indefinitely to examine your claims if they think you are committing fraud. Do you really want to worry every time you get a notice from the government in the mail or have to hold your breath every time you file a tax return? Not worth it — trust me!

What Is Tax Integration?

Tax integration is a concept that tax authorities use to try to ensure that the total tax burden is the same, regardless of the form of business ownership. Let's say you have a corporation and are taxed on the income coming in to the corporation. You then pay yourself a dividend. Therefore, there will be tax implications to the corporation and tax implications to you personally. Integration tries to make sure that the total tax the government receives is the same whether your business is a corporation, a partnership, or sole proprietorship.

Integration is not perfect, and this is where your accountant comes in. Governments change tax rates on both personal and corporate income for various reasons. They may want to create jobs or stimulate the economy. These tax changes may create opportunities for tax planning for the small business owner.

Annually, you should meet with your accountant to discuss any changes in tax law that will benefit you. You also want to be certain that the business structure you have created is still favorable to your particular tax situation.

Why You Need to Understand Tax Brackets

Most jurisdictions tax progressively. The more income you have, the higher your tax rate. Let's look at an example (note: these numbers are fictitious):

Income	Tax Rate
0 – 6,000	10%
6,001 – 27,950	15%
27,951 – 67,700	27%
67,701 – 141,250	30%
Over 141,250	35%

The income ranges on the left are called brackets. The rate corresponding to that bracket is the tax rate only on income inside that bracket. Let's say you had taxable income of $46,000 in a year. Under the above tax regime, your tax would be —

On the first 6,000 (6,000 X 10%)	$600.00
On 27,950 – 6,000 (21,950 X 15%)	3,292.50
On 46,000 – 27,950 (18,050 X 27%)	4,873.50
Total tax	**$8,766.00**

Note that the higher rates apply only to the income in that bracket. Many people think, for example, that the 27 percent rate would apply to the entire $46,000. If you've ever heard anyone say something like "There's no point in me working overtime. They take more tax than the extra I make," you're listening to a person who doesn't understand brackets. Although you get to keep progressively less of each extra dollar you make, you will always keep some.

The same concept applies to corporations. Up to a certain income level, most small businesses get a preferential tax rate. On income over these levels, they pay a higher rate of tax.

The art of tax minimization involves finding the right blend of taxation between the corporation and you as its owner. You want to structure your situation so that you pay the least amount of tax in total.

Deferring Tax Owing versus Getting Rid of It Altogether

There are two ways to minimize taxes for either yourself personally or your business: put them off until later or get rid of them altogether.

An example of a way to put them off until later is the use of a 401k (or, in Canada, an RRSP). If you put money into a 401k during the year, you can deduct it from your taxable income. For example, if you have $40,000 in income for the year and you put $10,000 into your 401k, you will be taxed on only $30,000. Sounds great! However, when you retire, you start to withdraw that money (along with all the investment growth), and at that point you will be taxed on that income.

So these types of plans only help you put off paying tax until later. That's still good, though. Tax later is almost always better than tax now.

What's preferable, though, is a permanent reduction of income taxes. There are many ways you can accomplish this:

1. *Make sure that you are tracking all your business expenses.* For example, if you are paying a lot of small things out of your own pocket on behalf of the company and losing the receipts, you are also losing the opportunity to pay less tax by claiming the expense. Although each individual receipt may not be for much, in total it may add up to significant lost dollars.
2. *Take advantage of all applicable government grants and incentives.* Many jurisdictions provide cash or tax incentives to small businesses to help stimulate the economy. Make sure that you are aware of these and are using them to their full advantage.
3. *Make sure you are using available tax exemptions.* For example, if your wife works full time in the business, make sure that she is being paid enough to "use up" her lower tax brackets. In most jurisdictions, income of spouse and children has to be commensurate with the actual work they are doing, but you still have some discretion in how much to pay them.

Owner/Manager Remuneration: Getting Money out of Your Business

Now that you've learned a little about taxes, it's time to talk about getting money from your business into your personal bank account.

If your business is a partnership or a sole proprietorship, it's easy. You simply write yourself a check. You can draw as much or as little as you like. It really doesn't matter from a tax perspective, because you will be taxed on the net income from the business before your draw. Let's look at an example:

Sole Proprietorship	
Revenue	$75,000
Expenses	(47,000)
Net income	**$28,000**

You will take the $28,000 into your taxable income on your personal income taxes regardless of what you did with that $28,000. It could still be sitting in the business bank account or you could have spent it on Beanie Babies. You're still taxed on the $28,000.

If you own a corporation, the situation is a little different. A corporation is a legal entity separate from you, and you therefore must formalize the payment of money into your pocket.

Earlier chapters discussed dividends and salary, the two ways that you can take money from your business. You can't just borrow it from the business and never pay it back. The tax authorities will eventually catch up with you and tax you on it.

You must examine the decision on whether to take salary or dividends from the corporation in light of the tax consequences involved. Salary is deducted in the corporation but fully taxed in your hands. Dividends are paid out of after-tax income from the business but taxed more favorably to the shareholder. There are also issues regarding having room to contribute to your personal retirement plan and for paying premiums to pension plans.

Again, sit down with your accountant annually and review your remuneration package from a taxation point of view.

Chapter Summary

- Good tax planning can make a significant difference in the amount of money you get to keep from your business.
- Tax minimization is good, but tax avoidance is illegal and can land you in jail.
- Tax integration is the government's attempt at making sure that it collects the same amount of tax, regardless of how you structure your affairs.
- Meet with your accountant annually to plan your taxation strategy; your accountant knows all the loopholes of the tax integration system.

Chapter 24

Graduation

You're finally here: at the end. You've looked at many bookkeeping issues, from setting up the books to handling the regular operating cycle of your business, to understanding some of the more complex issues your business may face.

You're well on your way to running your business more efficiently and effectively. But, this is a boot camp, and what would a boot camp be without a final test of your knowledge and prowess?

There is one boot camp question for every chapter. Take your time and work through the problems. If you get bogged down in a particular area, go back and read the chapter again, then retry the question.

The answers to the boot camp test are at the end of this chapter — but no cheating! If you've come this far, you have the skills to complete the test. Good luck, and I'll see you in the next book in the *Numbers 101 for Small Business* series, titled *Financial Management 101: Get a Grip on Your Business Numbers.*

Boot Camp Test

1. Chapter 2: A Brief Look at the Origins of Bookkeeping

What two critical advances had to exist before double-entry bookkeeping came into being?

____

____

2. Chapter 3: Important Concepts

Who are the four major groups of users of financial statements?

____

____

____

____

3. Chapter 4: Setting up the Record Keeping System

For each item, circle either the word "debit" or the word "credit."

Increases in asset accounts are debits/credits.

Decreases in equity accounts are debits/credits.

Increases in liability accounts are debits/credits.

Decreases in income are debits/credits.

Decreases in expenses are debits/credits.

4. Chapter 5: The Balance Sheet

A balance sheet is a __________ in time of what a company __________ and __________. Most items are recorded at ____________________ cost, but some are recorded at lower cost and __________________ and some at the ______________ of future cash flows. The fundamental accounting equation says:

____

Assets are sorted into three main categories: ________________, ________________, and ______________. Liabilities are split into two main categories: ______________ and ____.

Goodwill represents ____.

5. Chapter 6: The Income Statement

An income statement shows a company's ______________________________ over the period of time leading up to the related balance sheet. The income statement is split between income from operations and ______________________________________.

The statement of retained earnings represents a ________________________ of the changes in the retained earnings account.

6. Chapter 7: The Cash Flow Statement

The cash flow statement is the only one of the three main financial statements that deals with cash ____________________ and ________________________.

Here is the comparative balance sheet and income statement for Jessica Designs Inc. for the year ended 29 February 2008. Complete the cash flow statement.

Jessica Designs Inc.
Balance Sheet
29 February

	2008	2007
Assets		
Current		
Bank	$(15,242)	$9,720
Accounts receivable	1,923	2,410
Inventory	2,998	976
	$(10,321)	**$13,106**
Capital assets	43,897	47,812
Other assets	338	375
Total assets	**$33,914**	**$61,293**
Liabilities		
Current		
Accounts payable	$10,961	$12,475
Government remittances	653	592
Income taxes	112	97
Due to shareholder	4,836	6,502
	$16,562	**$19,666**
Long Term		
Mortgage payable	32,198	49,615
	48,760	69,281
Shareholders' equity		
Deficit	$(14,946)	$(8,088)
Capital stock	100	100
Total liabilities and equity	**$33,914**	**$61,293**

Jessica Designs Inc.
Statement of Income
For the Year Ended 29 February 2008

Revenue	$53,510
Cost of sales	27,212
Gross margin	**26,298**
Expenses	
Advertising	653
Bank charges	94
Depreciation	6,162
Office expenses	796
Professional fees	412
Supplies	524
Telephone & utilities	986
Vehicle expenses	478
Wages	3,673
	13,778
Net earnings before taxes	12,520
Income taxes	3,130
Net income	**$9,390**

Jessica Designs Inc.
Statement of Cash Flows
Year ended 29 February 2008

Net income	$ ______
Add back: Depreciation	______
	______
Cash from operating activities	
______ in Accounts receivable	______
______ in Inventory	______
______ in Accounts payable	______
______ in Gov't remittances	______
______ in Income taxes	______
______ in Due to shareholder	______
______ in Mortgage payable	______
	______

Cash from investing activities	
Purchase of capital assets	________________
	________________
Cash from financing activities	
Dividends	________________
	________________
Total __________ in cash	________________
Opening cash balance	________________
Closing cash balance	________________

7. Chapter 8: Recording the Sales Cycle

On March 15, 2008, Jessica Designs Inc. shipped a container of pillows to a customer in Mexico. The goods were received by the customer on March 21, 2008. The total billing to the customer was $1,475 (no taxes). The goods were shipped FOB destination. The terms of the billing were 2/10 net 30. The customer paid in 10 days and took the discount.

a) On what date does Jessica Designs Inc. record the sale?

b) Prepare the general journal entry to record the sale.

c) Prepare the general journal entry to record the cash receipt.

8. Chapter 9: Recording the Purchases Cycle

On March 27, 2008, Jessica Designs Inc. took possession of inventory with a total cost of $17,281 that had been shipped FOB destination. The terms were net 30, with interest at 2 percent per month for every month or part month late. The accounts payable clerk has been off sick for a few weeks and the invoice was not paid until May 10, 2008.

a) Prepare the purchase entry as if the company used the periodic inventory method.

b) Prepare the purchase entry as if the company used the perpetual inventory method.

c) Prepare the entry to record the payment of the invoice, including the interest.

9. Chapter 10: Inventory

Jessica Designs Inc. purchases bolts of material frequently to fill their custom upholstery orders. Their premium upholstery costs them the same amount regardless of the color or style. During the year, the company made the following purchases of premium upholstery material:

January 12	17 yards at $12.15/yard
March 26	24 yards at $13.47/yard
June 15	6 yards at $13.10/yard
September 30	16 yards at $14.98/yard
November 14	7 yards at $13.16/yard

The company started the year with no inventory of premium upholstery material. It uses the periodic inventory method. At year end, the controller performs an inventory count and calculates that there are 27 yards left in inventory. At what value will the company record the inventory on its balance sheet if —

a) It uses the FIFO method?

b) It uses the LIFO method?

c) It uses the average cost method?

10. Chapter 11: Capital Assets

Jessica Designs Inc. purchased an industrial sewing and cutting machine for $4,500. The company paid $65 in shipping costs to have it delivered to the plant and paid an electrician $175 to install and test the machine. The machine will be depreciated at 20 percent declining balance.

a) Prepare the purchase entry.

b) Prepare the depreciation entry at the end of the first year.

11. Chapter 12: Leases and Loans

Jessica Designs Inc. entered into a lease for a delivery truck. The value of the truck is $27,625, and 60 monthly lease payments of $517 must be made. Record the entry to set up the lease if —

a) The lease is a capital lease.

b) The lease is an operating lease.

12. Chapter 13: Transactions between the Company and Its Owners

a) The owner of Jessica Designs Inc., Jessica Taylor, bought supplies totaling $127.83 on her personal credit card. The supplies were for the business. Record the entry.

b) The company accrues a bonus payable for Jessica in the amount of $3,000. Record the entry.

c) Jessica uses her personally owned car 65 percent for business purposes. Her total vehicle expenses for the year were:

Fuel	1,475
Repairs	675
Lease	8,750
Insurance	795
Licence	85

Prepare the entry to record the business usage of the car in the company.

13. Chapter 14: Remittances to the Government

Jessica Designs Inc. is a Canadian company and, as such, must collect and remit Goods and Services Tax (GST) to Canada Revenue Agency. On January 22nd, the company prepares an invoice for a customer in the amount of $1,745 plus 5 percent GST.

Prepare the journal entry to record the sale.

The company also has several employees. The following information relates to the January 15th pay of one of the employees.

Gross pay	$1,350.00
CPP withheld	89.46
EI withheld	47.12
Income tax	476.11
Net pay	$737.31

The company must match the employee's CPP withholdings and must contribute 1.4 times the employee's EI withholdings. Prepare the entry to record the payroll check.

14. Chapter 15: Maintaining a Petty Cash System

JDI needs to cut a check to top up its petty cash fund. The fund started at an even $100 on January 10. The receipts and the cash left in the box total to the $100. The following is found in the box.

Receipts:

Office supplies	$27.30 (subtotal $26.00 with GST of $1.30)
Muffins	12.08 (subtotal 11.50 with GST of 0.58)
Courier	23.42 (subtotal of 22.30 with GST of 1.12)
Postage	35.18 (subtotal of 33.50 with GST of 1.68)

Cash:

Change	$2.02

Prepare the general journal entry to record the check written to top up petty cash.

15. Chapter 16: Reconciling the Bank

JDI opened a new US dollar bank account at the beginning of January to facilitate payment by their US customers. The bank activity in their general journal looked like this:

Date	Description	DR	CR	Balance
4 Jan	Initial deposit	400.00		400.00
6 Jan	Ck #1 Olam's Mfg.		213.45	186.55
9 Jan	Deposit	1,753.00		1,939.55
14 Jan	Ck #2 Marcell Designs		617.71	1,321.84
17 Jan	Ck #3 Artco		391.85	929.99
25 Jan	Deposit	475.96		1,405.95
25 Jan	Ck #4 Carson Int'l		97.35	1,308.60
31 Jan	Deposit	219.75		1,528.35

The bank statement for JDI's new account arrives on February 14th. It provides the following information:

Date	Description	DR	CR	Balance
5 Jan	Deposit	400.00		400.00
10 Jan	Deposit	1,753.00		2,153.00
17 Jan	Ck #3		391.85	1,761.15
12 Jan	Ck #1		213.45	1,547.70
14 Jan	Ck #2		617.71	929.99
26 Jan	Deposit	475.96		1,405.95
31 Jan	Account fees		27.95	1,378.00

Prepare the bank reconciliation for January:

16. Chapter 17: When the Damn Thing Just Won't Balance

Transposition errors are always divisible by ____________________.

Backwards posting errors are always divisible by __________________.

Addition errors are usually ________________________________.

17. Chapter 18: When Your Books Are Already a Mess

Organize your bookkeeping for the future. Revisit Step 7 in Chapter 18 for some self-reflection.

18. Chapter 19: The Role of the External Accountant

Using the JDI income statement in Question 6, prepare the closing entry.

19. Chapter 20: Budgeting: Planning for the Future

JDI is starting the budgeting process for the year ending February 28, 2009. The monthly income statement for the 2008 year end looks like this:

Jessica Design Inc.
MONTHLY INCOME STATEMENT
Year ended 29 February 2008

Month	Mar	Apr	May	Jun	Jul	Aug	Sep	Oct	Nov	Dec	Jan	Feb	Total
Revenue	3,725	4,612	4,109	3,289	5,085	5,139	4,103	3,578	3,945	4,210	6,412	5,303	$53,510
COGS	1,895	2,416	1,989	1,675	2,756	2,708	1,965	1,792	2,006	2,165	3,260	2,585	27,212
Advertising	50	50	50	50	50	50	103	50	50	50	50	50	653
Bank charges	7	7	7	7	7	7	7	7	7	7	7	17	94
Office expenses	61	68	66	72	69	65	73	57	53	65	76	71	796
Professional fees	0	0	0	412	0	0	0	0	0	0	0	0	412
Supplies	39	31	42	19	65	58	17	39	42	58	63	51	524
Telephone & utilities	87	89	79	96	85	89	97	89	71	69	59	76	986
Vehicle expenses	39	47	32	45	49	51	34	31	32	41	39	38	478
Wages	306	310	285	296	314	312	342	284	292	325	312	295	3,673
Net income	1,241	1,594	1,559	617	1,690	1,799	1,465	1,229	1,392	1,430	2,546	2,120	18,682

The following information is relevant to the budgeting process:

- Revenues are expected to increase by 10 percent next year.
- JDI has found a new supplier. The Cost of Goods Sold savings should be 3 percent.
- Advertising rates have increased for the upcoming year by 5 percent.
- Vehicle expenses in the past have represented actual fuel and repairs on the employee's vehicle. This year, the employees will be reimbursed at $0.36 per mile. It is expected that there will be a total of 1,250 miles driven in the upcoming year. These will be spread evenly over the months.
- JDI will have to hire a new part-time employee for the upcoming year to handle the projected increase in sales. The projected increase in wages and benefits is $3,675, spread evenly over the months.

Prepare the budget for the 2008 year end.

20. Chapter 21: Monitoring Cash Flow: How Not to Run out of Money

The difference between cash flow and net income is ______________________________.

Name four ways to stretch your cash flow further:

____

____

____

____

21. Chapter 22: A Brief Look at Foreign Currency

JDI purchased inventory from a US supplier on February 10. The amount of the invoice was $1,975 USD. The average exchange rate for February was 1.57. The exchange rate on February 29 was 1.59. The invoice was paid in March from the US dollar bank account. The average exchange rate for March was 1.62.

a) Prepare the general journal entry to record the purchase of inventory.

b) Prepare the general journal entry to record the year end revaluation of US accounts payable.

Jessica Design Inc.
BUDGETED INCOME STATEMENT
Year ended 28 February 2008

Month	Mar	Apr	May	Jun	Jul	Aug	Sep	Oct	Nov	Dec	Jan	Feb	Total
Revenue													
COGS													
Advertising													
Bank charges													
Office expenses													
Professional fees													
Supplies													
Telephone & utilities													
Vehicle expenses													
Wages													
Net income													

c) Prepare the general journal entry to record the payment of the invoice.

22. Chapter 23: Tax Planning

The following income tax rates apply to individuals.

0 - 5,000	7%
5,001 - 12,500	14%
12,501 - 21,000	31%
over 21,000	36%

If an individual made $32,000 in taxable income in a year, how much income tax would he or she have to pay?

Boot Camp Test Answers

1. Chapter 2: A Brief Look at the Origins of Bookkeeping

What two critical advances had to exist before double-entry bookkeeping came into being?

the invention of coinage

the development of the Arabic numbering system

2. Chapter 3: Important Concepts

Who are the four major groups of users of financial statements?

Owners

Investors

Lenders

Tax authorities

3. Chapter 4: Setting up the Record Keeping System

For each item, circle either the word "debit" or the word "credit."

Increases in asset accounts are (debits)/ credits.

Decreases in equity accounts are (debits)/ credits.

Increases in liability accounts are debits /(credits).

Decreases in income are (debits)/ credits.

Decreases in expenses are debits /(credits).

4. **Chapter 5: The Balance Sheet**

A balance sheet is a __snapshot__ in time of what a company __owns__ and __owes__. Most items are recorded at __historical__ cost, but some are recorded at lower cost and __market__ and some at the __present value__ of future cash flows.

The fundamental accounting equation says:

__ASSETS = LIABILITIES + OWNERS'S EQUITY__

Assets are sorted into three main categories: __current__, __capital__, and ______. Liabilities are split into two main categories: __current__ and __long term__.

Goodwill represents __the value of a business that doesn't relate to its hard assets__.

5. **Chapter 6: The Income Statement**

An income statement shows a company's __operating activity__ over the period of time leading up to the related balance sheet. The income statement is split between income from operations and __extraordinary items__.

The statement of retained earnings represents a __reconciliation__ of the changes in the retained earnings account.

6. **Chapter 7: The Cash Flow Statement**

The cash flow statement is the only one of the three main financial statements that deals with cash __inflows__ and __outflows__.

Here is the comparative balance sheet and income statement for Jessica Designs Inc. for the year ended 29 February 2008. Complete the cash flow statement.

Jessica Designs Inc.
Statement of Cash Flows
Year ended 29 February 2008

Net income	$9,390
Add back: Depreciation	6,162
	15,552
Cash from operating activities	
Decrease in Accounts receivable	487
Increase in Inventory	(2,022)
Decrease in Accounts payable	(1,514)
Increase in Gov't remittances	61
Increase in Income taxes	15

Increase in Due to shareholder	(1,666)
Decrease in Mortgage payable	(17,417)
	(6,504)
Cash from investing activities	
Purchase of capital assets	(2,210)
	(2,210)
Cash from financing activities	
Dividends	(16,248)
	(16,248)
Total Decrease in cash	(24,962)
Opening cash balance	9,720
Closing cash balance	(15,242)

7. **Chapter 8: Recording the Sales Cycle**

a) On what date does Jessica Designs Inc. record the sale?

21 March 2008

b) Prepare the general journal entry to record the sale.

DR	Accounts receivable	$1,475.00	
CR	Sales		$1,475.00

c) Prepare the general journal entry to record the cash receipt.

DR	Cash	$1,445.50	
DR	Sales discounts	29.50	
CR	Accounts receivable		$1,475.00

8. **Chapter 9: Recording the Purchases Cycle**

a) Prepare the purchase entry as if the company used the periodic inventory method.

DR	Purchases	$17,281.00	
CR	Accounts payable		$17,281.00

b) Prepare the purchase entry as if the company used the perpetual inventory method.

DR	Purchases	$17,281.00	
CR	Accounts payable		$17,281.00

c) Prepare the entry to record the payment of the invoice, including the interest.

DR	Accounts payable	$17,281.00	
DR	Internet expense	345.62	
CR	Cash		$17,626.62

9. Chapter 10: Inventory

At what value will the company record the inventory on its balance sheet if —

a) It uses the FIFO method?
$384.20

b) It uses the LIFO method?
$341.25

c) It uses the average cost method?
$362.61

10. Chapter 11: Capital Assets

a) Prepare the purchase entry.

DR	Equipment	$4,740.00	
CR	Accounts payable (or cash)		$4,740.00

b) Prepare the depreciation entry at the end of the first year.

DR	Depreciation expense	$948.00	
CR	Accumulated Dep'n-Equipment		$948.00

11. Chapter 12: Leases and Loans

Record the entry to set up the lease if —

a) The lease is a capital lease.

DR	Vehicle	$27,625.00	
CR	Capital lease obligation		$27,625.00

b) The lease is an operating lease.

There is no entry required to set up an operating lease. (Sorry, we needed at least one trick question!)

12. Chapter 13: Transactions between the Company and Its Owners

a) The owner of Jessica Designs Inc., Jessica Taylor, bought supplies totaling $127.83 on her personal credit card. The supplies were for the business. Record the entry.

DR	Supplies	$127.83	
CR	Due to shareholder		$127.83

b) The company accrues a bonus payable for Jessica in the amount of $3,000. Record the entry.

DR	Wages	$3,000.00	
CR	Management bonus payable		$3,000.00

c) Prepare the entry to record the business usage of the car in the company.

Total expenses = $11,780
Business usage = $11,780 X 65% = $7,657

DR	Equipment	$4,740.00	
CR	Accounts payable (or cash)		$4,740.00

13. Chapter 14: Remittances to the Government

Prepare the journal entry to record the sale.

DR	Accounts receivable	$1,849.70	
CR	Sales		$1,745.00
CR	GST collected		104.70

Prepare the entry to record the payroll check.

First calculate the employer's payroll expense:

Employee CPP X 1.0 = 89.46

Employee EI X 1.4 = 65.97

Total employer expenses = 155.43

DR	Wages	$1,350.00	
DR	Payroll expenses	155.43	
CR	Payroll liabilities		$768.12
CR	Cash		737.31

14. Chapter 15: Maintaining a Petty Cash System

Prepare the general journal entry to record the check written to top up petty cash.

DR	Office supplies	$26.00
DR	Postage	33.50
DR	Courier	22.30
DR	Miscellaneous	11.50
DR	GST paid	5.48
CR	Cash	$98.78

15. Chapter 16: Reconciling the Bank

Prepare the bank reconciliation for January:

First record the entry for bank charges:

DR	Bank charges	$27.95
CR	Cash	$27.95

The new cash balance is therefore (1,528.35 – 27.95) = 1,500.40

Balance per bank	1,378.00
Less: outstanding check	
#4 Carson Int'l	(97.35)
Add: outstanding deposit	
31 January	219.75
Balance per books	$1,500.40

16. Chapter 17: When the Damn Thing Just Won't Balance

Transposition errors are always divisible by ___9___.

Backwards posting errors are always divisible by ___2___.

Addition errors are usually ___round numbers___.

17. Chapter 18: When Your Books Are Already a Mess

Organize your bookkeeping for the future. Revisit Step 7 in Chapter 18 for some self-reflection.

Disorganization can result in something as small as lost profits and late payment fees, or it can prove disastrous for my company's financial integrity. By keeping my books organized, I may be able to increase profits, change my company's market when required, and save hundreds by paying my bills on time. If I don't have the time or interest to organize my company's books, I can hire an accountant. Despite that accounting services cost money, these costs may be counteracted by the profits I'll gain just by getting organized.

18. Chapter 19: The Role of the External Accountant

Using the JDI income statement in Question 6, prepare the closing entry.

DR	Revenue	$53,510.00	
CR	COGS		$27,212.00
CR	Advertising		653.00
CR	Bank charges		94.00
CR	Depreciation		6,162.00
CR	Office expenses		796.00
CR	Professional fees		412.00
CR	Supplies		524.00
CR	Telephone & utilities		986.00
CR	Vehicle expenses		478.00
CR	Wages		3,673.00
CR	Income tax expense		3,130.00
CR	Retained earnings		9,390.00

19. Chapter 20: Budgeting: Planning for the Future

JDI is starting the budgeting process for the year ending February 28, 2008. Prepare the budget for the 2008 year end.

Jessica Design Inc.
BUDGETED INCOME STATEMENT
Year ended 28 February 2008

Month	Mar	Apr	May	Jun	Jul	Aug	Sep	Oct	Nov	Dec	Jan	Feb	Total
Revenue	4,098	5,073	4,520	3,618	5,594	5,653	4,513	3,936	4,340	4,631	7,053	5,833	**58,862**
COGS	1,838	2,344	1,929	1,625	2,673	2,627	1,906	1,738	1,946	2,100	3,162	2,507	**26,395**
Advertising	53	53	53	53	53	53	108	53	53	53	53	53	**691**
Bank charges	7	7	7	7	7	7	7	7	7	7	7	17	**94**
Office expenses	61	68	66	72	69	65	73	57	53	65	76	71	**796**
Professional fees	0	0	0	412	0	0	0	0	0	0	0	0	**412**
Supplies	39	31	42	19	65	58	17	39	42	58	63	51	**524**
Telephone & utilities	87	89	79	96	85	89	97	89	71	69	59	76	**986**
Vehicle expenses	38	38	38	38	38	38	38	38	38	38	38	38	**456**
Wages	612	616	591	602	620	618	648	590	598	631	618	601	**7,345**
Net income	1,363	1,827	1,715	694	1,984	2,098	1,619	1,325	1,532	1,610	2,977	2,419	21,163

20. Chapter 21: Monitoring Cash Flow: How Not to Run out of Money

The difference between cash flow and net income is Cash flow represents cash inflows and outflows, regardless of source, whereas net income represents the accrued results of a company's operations.

Name four ways to stretch your cash flow further:

Collect receivables earlier

Pay payables at the farthest date possible without penalty

Buy inventory only as needed

Barter business services with other business owners

21. Chapter 22: A Brief Look at Foreign Currency

a) Prepare the general journal entry to record the purchase of inventory.

DR	Purchases (or inventory)	$3,100.75	
CR	Accounts payable — US		$1,975.00
CR	Exchange on Accounts payable — US		1,125.75

b) Prepare the general journal entry to record the year end revaluation of US accounts payable.

DR	Foreign exchange gain/loss	$39.50	
CR	Exchange on Accounts payable — US		$39.50

c) Prepare the general journal entry to record the payment of the invoice.

DR	Accounts payable — US	$1,975.00	
DR	Exchange on Accounts payable — US	1,165.25	
DR	Foreign exchange gain/loss	59.25	
CR	US Bank		$1,975.00
CR	Exchange on US bank		1,224.50

22. Chapter 23: Tax Planning

If an individual made $32,000 in taxable income in a year, how much income tax would he or she have to pay?

First 5,000	7%	$350
Next 7,500	14%	1,050
Next 8,000	31%	2,480
Next 11,000	36%	3,960
Total		**7,840**

Glossary

Accounting: The cyclical recording and reporting of a business's financial transactions and the analysis of the business's financial statements.

Accounts payable (also called trade payables): The amounts owed by a business to its suppliers or vendors for goods and services purchased on credit.

Accounts receivable: The amounts owed to a business from its customers for goods or services provided on credit.

Accrued liabilities (also called accrued expenses): The amounts owed by a business to its suppliers or employees that relate to the current period but for which it has not yet been invoiced.

Accumulated depreciation: The total amount of depreciation taken on a capital asset to date over its lifetime. The accumulated depreciation is recorded on the balance sheet as a contra account (see definition below), reducing the total original cost of the asset. The net of the original cost and the accumulated depreciation is known as the net book value of the capital asset.

Accrual accounting: A method of accounting in which income and expenses are recorded in the periods in which they occur, not necessarily the periods in which cash is exchanged. Accrual accounting is based on the matching principle.

Allowance for doubtful accounts (AFDA): A balance sheet account that captures management's best estimate of the total of the potentially uncollectible accounts receivable at any particular point in time. AFDA is a contra account to the accounts receivable account.

Asset: Something owned is of measurable value to the owner both in the present as well as in future periods.

Auditor: An accountant outside of a business who performs specific procedures to give the users of the financial statements comfort regarding the accuracy and completeness of the numbers.

Audit report: The single-page statement prepared by an auditor summarizing the audit procedures performed, the scope of the audit, and the opinion of the auditor regarding the accuracy and completeness of the numbers.

Bad debts: The estimated amount of credit sales that have become questionable as to collectibility in the current period.

Balance sheet: One of the three major financial statements of a business. The balance sheet displays everything of a measurable financial value that is owned and owed by the company.

Bank reconciliation: The process of comparing and reporting differences between the bank balance on the bank statement and the bank balance in the ledger.

Book value: The value of assets, liabilities, and equity recorded on the balance sheet of a business. Book value may differ (sometimes substantially) from replacement cost or market value.

Budgeting: The process of planning and projecting revenues, expenses, and capital expenditures for future fiscal periods.

Capital assets: The tangible operating assets of a business. These assets generally provide the business with operating capacity as opposed to being held for resale. They have a relatively long life.

Capital lease obligations: The present value of all amounts owing under a capital lease contract. A capital lease is a lease in which the rights and responsibilities of ownership have passed to the lessee.

Capital stock: The units of ownership of a corporation, issued by certificate.

Cash basis accounting: A method of accounting in which financial transactions are recognized in the period in which cash transfers, not necessarily the period to which that event relates. This method is generally not allowed by generally accepted accounting principles (GAAP).

Cash flow: The inflows to and outflows from a business, regardless of the source.

Cash flow statement (also known as the statement of changes in financial position): One of the three major financial statements of a business. The cash flow statement, in its most general terms, shows why there is an increase or decrease in cash during the year. These increases and decreases are summarized into operating, financing, and investing activities.

Certified Public Accountant (CPA): A widely recognized professional accounting designation in the United States. To be a CPA, one must meet educational and experience requirements, as well as pass a uniform examination to qualify for a state license to practice.

Chartered Accountant (CA): A widely recognized professional accounting designation in Canada, the UK, and Australia. A CA must meet educational and experience requirements and pass a uniform examination to be able to hold a public accounting license. Requirements vary between the countries as the designation is administered by different professional regulatory bodies.

Certified Management Accountant (CMA): A professional accounting designation widely recognized in the United States and Canada. CMAs must also pass rigorous standards before attaining the designation; however, the focus of training is more on internal management practices as opposed to public accounting.

Certified General Accountant (CGA): Another professional accounting designation in Canada that requires candidates to meet certain standards before being granted the designation.

Chart of accounts: The set of accounts used by a business that make up its general ledger. These accounts are standard to that particular organization, and all transactions must be recorded using these standard accounts unless a change is granted by management.

Closing the books: The process of ending the accounting period (usually the year) in which the balances of all revenue and expense accounts are transferred to increase or decrease the retained earnings balance. The closing procedure allows the income statement to "start fresh" for the new year.

Common stock: Represents the controlling shares of the company. The common stockholders are usually the only shareholders who have the right to vote on issues important to the survival and direction of the corporation. Common stock is required to be issued by the corporation (someone has to control the company). Upon the dissolution of the corporation, the common shareholders are generally the last to receive any net assets of the company.

Compound interest: Interest earned on your interest. You earn compound interest when you leave your interest in an investment. During the next period, you earn interest on both your principal and the reinvested interest.

Contra account: An account that nets off the balance of another account.

Controller (comptroller): The "big cheese" accountant in an organization. The controller oversees all accounting functions and sometimes operates as the company's chief financial officer.

Cooking the books: The process of making the financial results look pretty. Although there are many acceptable choices that can be made with respect to accounting policies, "cooking the books" generally involves fraudulent methods of recording non-existent transactions or transactions with values different from what is being recorded.

Corporation: One of the three main forms of business ownership (sole proprietorship and partnership are the other two). A corporation is the only type of business entity that is legally separate from its owners: it is itself a legal entity. Corporate ownership is shown through the issue of share certificates (see *Common stock*).

Cost accounting: An older term for management accounting. Cost accounting is usually more narrowly defined as accounting for the costs of manufacturing goods and apportioning them to the correct products in the correct periods.

Cost of goods sold (COGS): The purchase or manufacturing costs of the goods that were sold during a particular period. The costs related to the goods not yet sold are accounted for in inventory on the balance sheet.

Creditor: A person or other entity that has loaned money or extended credit to a business.

Current assets: A category of assets on the balance sheet that represents cash and assets that are expected to be converted into cash within one year.

Current liabilities: A category of liabilities on the balance sheet that represents financial obligations that are expected to be settled within one year.

Debits and credits: Accounting terminology representing the increases and decreases in ledger accounts. Debits represent increases to assets and expenses, and decreases to liabilities, revenues, and equity accounts. Credits represent increases to liabilities, revenues and equity accounts, and decreases to assets and expenses.

Debt: The amounts owed by a business to outside persons or businesses. It is sometimes more narrowly defined as to exclude accounts payable and include only loans that have fixed interest rates and repayment schedules.

Declining balance method: An accelerated method of depreciation that results in more depreciation being taken in earlier periods.

Deferred revenue: Represents revenue received in advance of services performed or product delivered. It is a liability on the balance sheet because the business has an obligation to perform the service or deliver the product.

Depreciation expense: The portion of capital assets that have been recognized in expenses for the current operating period.

Dividends: The portion of earnings (either current or retained from prior periods) that have been distributed out to the shareholders in the current operating period.

Double-entry bookkeeping: The method of bookkeeping first documented in 1494 that recognizes that each financial transaction affects at least two balances simultaneously.

Double-declining balance method: Another accelerated depreciation method.

Earnings: A term usually used interchangeably with net income (i.e., revenues less expenses).

Extraordinary gains and losses: Increases or decreases in net income from sources not directly related to the operating capacity of the business. These are events that are not expected to recur.

Fair market value: An approximation of the worth of an asset if sold in an open market environment.

Financial Accounting Standards Board (FASB): The issuer of generally accepted accounting principles in the United States and its most authoritative standard-setting body.

Financial statements: The main summary financial reports produced by a business's accounting and bookkeeping system. The three major financial statements are the balance sheet, the income statement, and the cash flow statement.

Financing activities: One of the three major summary categories on the cash flow statement. Financing activities are those transactions between a business and its sources of funding. It includes the borrowing and repayment of debt, issue and retraction of share capital, and the payment of dividends.

First-in, first-out (FIFO): A method of inventory valuation by which the inventory items are tracked in and out in date order. When a sale is made, it is the cost of the oldest items in inventory that is applied to the cost of goods sold account, and it is the cost of the more recent purchases that remain in inventory.

Fixed assets: An older term for capital assets (see *Capital assets*).

FOB destination: A method of determining who owns goods in transit: the business or the business's customers or suppliers. If something is shipped FOB destination, title to the goods does not pass to the purchaser until the goods have reached the purchaser's premises.

FOB shipping point: A method of determining who owns goods in transit: the business or the business's customers or suppliers. If something is shipped FOB shipping point, title to the goods passes when the goods leave the vendor's premises.

General ledger: The grouping of accounts used by a business. Also, the book where the main summary records are kept for each balance sheet and income statement item.

General journal: A detailed record of all financial transactions of a business. The general journal is summarized and entered as net increases and decreases to the accounts in the general ledger.

Generally Accepted Accounting Principles (GAAP): The collection of standards and practices required to be used by businesses to record and present the results of their financial activities and their records of what they own and what they owe. GAAP can be different between industries and between countries.

Goods-in-process: A term used interchangeably with work-in-progress.

Goodwill: In the general sense, goodwill represents the intangible asset that a business possesses by virtue of its good name in the community, strong and loyal customer list, and brand-name recognition. In its more narrowly defined accounting sense, goodwill represents the intangible value that has been paid for when a company purchases another company. This is the only type of goodwill that generates accounting recognition. It is carried as an asset on the balance sheet.

Gross income: Another term for revenues.

Gross margin: Represents revenues minus the cost of goods sold in the period.

Income statement: One of the three major financial statements of a business. (The balance sheet and the cash flow statement are the other two.) The income statement shows operating activity over an operating period from revenues, expenses, and extraordinary gains and losses.

Income tax payable: The total of the income taxes that have not yet been remitted to the government but are due at the end of the year. This total would include income taxes in arrears if there were any.

Insolvent: A term used to describe a business that does not have enough assets to meet its debt obligations in the short term. Insolvency can lead to bankruptcy if not corrected quickly.

Internal control: Represents the procedures set up in a business to prevent errors and fraudulent activity.

Inventory: Goods held for resale that remain unsold at the end of an operating period. In a manufacturing environment, inventory includes raw materials, goods in the process of being made, and finished goods. In certain service industries, inventory includes time spent on customer activities but not yet billed out.

Investing activities: One of the three major summary categories on the cash flow statement. Investing activities include the purchase and sale of capital assets, including land, buildings, equipment, and furniture and fixtures.

Investments: Usually, long-term investments in other companies, as opposed to the short-term re-investment of excess operating funds.

Last-in, first-out (LIFO): A method of inventory valuation by which the inventory items are tracked in and out in the date order. When a sale is made, it is the cost of the newest items in inventory that is applied to cost of goods sold account, and it is the cost of the oldest purchases that remain in inventory. Note that some taxation authorities do not allow this method. Check with your accountant.

Lease obligation: See *Capital lease obligations*.

Liability: Something that is owed by the business to outside parties. Liabilities can be current or long-term, depending on when the obligation is to be settled.

Limited liability company (LLC): A newer form of business ownership in the United States that carries with it characteristics of both a partnership and a corporation.

Limited liability partnership (LLP): A newer form of business ownership in Canada. Generally, it can be used only by professionals (accountants, lawyers, doctors). It has some benefit to the owners as it limits some of the normally unlimited liability of the partners.

Liquidity: The ability of an asset to convert into cash, or its ability to be easily sold. Assets are shown on the balance sheet in the order of their liquidity, the most liquid (cash) coming first.

Long-term liability: An obligation that is not expected to be settled within one year. The current portion of these liabilities (i.e., present value of payments due within one year) is shown in the current liability section of the balance sheet.

Lower of cost or market (LCM): A method of valuation usually applied only to inventories. Inventory must be recorded on the balance sheet at the lower value of its original cost or its value on the current market.

Management accounting: The accounting done internally to assist managers in their decision-making role. Management accounting encompasses budgeting, forecasting, unit costing, and ratio analysis.

Market value: See *Fair market value*.

Marketable securities: Investments (usually made with temporary excess operating funds) that are highly liquid, such as stocks, bonds, mutual funds, and income certificates. Marketable securities are presented on the balance sheet as current assets, as usually they will be converted to cash within one year.

Matching principle: One of the fundamental accounting principles that states that expenses should be matched to the revenues to which they relate.

Meals and entertainment: An important category of expenses, meals and entertainment usually attracts separate taxation treatment.

Mortgage payable: The balance of a business's debt that is secured by the business's real property. The most common reason for the borrowing is the purchase of land and buildings in which the business will operate. The present value of the mortgage payments due within one year are presented in current liabilities on the balance sheet, and the present value of the payments due more than one year out are presented in the long-term liability section.

MYOB: *Mind Your Own Business,* a popular accounting software program for small businesses.

Net book value: The difference between the original cost of a capital asset and its accumulated depreciation.

Net income: The income left in an accounting period after all expenses have been deducted from revenues. The term net income is used only if the revenues exceed the expenses.

Net loss: The deficit for an accounting period that occurs when the expenses for that period exceed the revenues.

Note receivable: An amount backed by a promissory note to be paid to a business.

Obsolescence: Usually used in reference to inventory, obsolescence is the loss in use of an item due to new and improved items taking its place, changes in customer preference, or other conditions unrelated to the physical condition of the item.

Operating activities: Those activities in which a business engages that create its main source of profit.

Operating cycle: The period of time it takes for a business to complete a full round of its operating activity. It is the time it takes to convert cash back into cash, which includes buying inventory, selling inventory, and collecting the receivables.

Owners' equity: The amounts owed by a business to its owners rather than outside parties.

Partnership: One of the three main forms of business ownership. A partnership is an unincorporated business with two or more owners. Partnerships are jointly owned by the partners and do not have a separate "legal life" of their own.

Periodic inventory: A method of accounting for inventory by which all purchases throughout the operating cycle are posted to cost of goods sold. Inventory is physically counted at the end of the period, and the adjustment for goods sold is made at that point. With this method, inventory is correct only at the end of the period.

Perpetual inventory: A method of accounting for inventory by which goods are recorded as being removed from inventory as they are sold. With this method, inventory is always theoretically correct and is checked against a physical count at the end of the period.

Posting: The process of summarizing general journal entries and recording them in the general ledger.

Preferred stock: Shares of a corporation that in the event of a dissolution of the corporation, entitle their holders to receive dividends and net assets of the corporation in preference to the common shares.

Prepaid expenses: Expenses that have been paid in the current period but which relate to future periods. Prepaid expenses appear as current assets on the balance sheet.

Profit: See *Net Income.*

Profit and loss (P&L) statement: Another name for an income statement.

QuickBooks: A popular accounting software program for small businesses.

Residual value: The amount that a capital asset is expected to be worth at the end of its useful life with the corporation.

Retained earnings: The amount of cumulative net income that remains in the business that has not been paid out to the owners.

Revenue: The amount of net assets generated by a business as a result of its operations.

Service life: The period of time over which a capital asset is expected to be useful to a business.

Shareholder: An owner or internal investor of a corporation.

Simply Accounting: A popular accounting software program for small businesses.

Sole proprietorship: One of the three major forms of business ownership. A sole proprietorship is an unincorporated company owned by a single owner. It has no "legal life" of its own.

Solvency: The ability of a company to settle its liabilities with its assets.

Statement of cash flows: One of the three major financial statements. The statement of cash flows explains the changes in assets, liabilities, and net equity for the period.

Statement of changes in financial position: An older term for the statement of cash flows.

Stockholder: See *Shareholder.*

Straight-line depreciation: A method of calculating depreciation of capital assets that results in an even amount of depreciation being expensed every period.

Sum of the years' digits method (SYD): A seldom-used method of accelerated depreciation that results in more depreciation being expensed in earlier years.

Taxable income: The amount of net income that is subject to income tax. It will differ from net income per the financial statements by any differences between GAAP and tax regulations.

Transaction: A financial event that is recorded in a business's books.

Working papers: A set of documents prepared for the external accountants to verify the balances and calculations made in a business's books.

Writedown: An accounting entry to reduce the carrying value of an asset, such as inventory, to its market value.

Write off: A slang term for expensing a cost in the books of a business.

Appendix

B

Resources for the Growing Business

www.numbers101.com

Our official website that is packed full of articles, advice, and business tools such as cash flow spreadsheets, templates, and links.

www.aicpa.org

The official website of the American Institute of Certified Public Accountants. Here you can find out what qualifications CPAs are required to have and how to find a CPA in your state.

www.cica.ca

The official website of the Canadian Institute of Chartered Accountants.

www.cma-canada.org

The official website of CMA Canada.

www.sba.gov

US Small Business Administration — lots of great resources for small businesses. Mostly US-focused but useful for all companies.

www.cfib.ca

Canadian Federation of Independent Business. CFIB is an advocacy group for small businesses. They lobby the government for legislative changes that will assist businesses and their owners. On the website are lease-versus-buy calculators, downloadable publications, and other resources.

http://sme.ic.gc.ca

Industry Canada. A great website for businesses from all countries. Shows you how your business stacks up with others in your industry.

www.toolkit.com

CCH Business Owner's Toolkit. Great tools and resources including sample business documents, checklists, and government forms.

www.inc.com

The online presence of *Inc. magazine.* Here you will find great articles, tools, and calculators to help your business grow.

www.self-counsel.com

Online shopping for a wide variety of business titles (including this one!).

Must-read Books

There are literally thousands of books on every aspect of business, from start-up to management to marketing. There are, however, some books that have stood the test of time, and which, in my humble opinion, should be rendered dog-eared and tattered by every small-business owner. You can buy these books at almost any bookstore, or you can visit www.numbers101.com to find links to an online retailer in your country. Please note: These books are not in any particular order.

Built to Last: Successful Habits of Visionary Companies by James C. Collins and Jerry I. Porras (New York: HarperBusiness, 2002)

This book looks at companies that have stood the test of time and that have not only survived but also flourished while their competitors have fallen by the wayside. Learn how you can structure your business the same way to ensure that it's around a hundred years from now.

The e-Myth Revisited: Why Most Small Businesses Don't Work and What to Do about It by Michael E. Gerber (New York, N.Y.: HarperBusiness, 1995)

This powerful book has changed the lives of hundreds of thousands of small-business owners. Gerber shows you that being able to do the things your business does (cut hair, design buildings, fly aircrafts) does not necessarily mean that you have the skills to manage a business. He shows you how to work on instead of just in your business.

Extraordinary Guarantees: Achieving Breakthrough Gains in Quality & Customer Satisfaction by Christopher W. Hart (New York: Amacom, 1993)

An unusual take on "the customer is always right" philosophy. This book looks at the benefits of making the buying decision risk-free for your customers.

Guerrilla Marketing: Secrets for Making Big Profits from Your Small Business by Jay Conrad Levinson (Boston: Houghton Mifflin, 1998)

Every business owner, large and small, wants information on how to market effectively at a low (or no) cost. This book, along with the others in the series, gives hands-on advice to readers on how to gain media attention and market their companies.

Marketing Your Services: For People Who Hate to Sell by Rick Crandall (New York: McGraw-Hill, 2002)

In my opinion, this is one of the best books on marketing services. It shows you how to focus on building relationships instead of selling. If you think you're paying too much for advertising space and you want to get "free" advertising, this is the book for you!

Multiple Streams of Income: How to Generate a Lifetime of Unlimited Wealth by Robert G. Allen (New York: John Wiley & Sons, 2000)

This book is applicable to all areas of a business owner's life. It takes a holistic view of the entrepreneur's life and shows the necessity of having several sources of income flowing into your bank account to help you survive financial risk.

The One-Minute Manager by Kenneth Blanchard and Spencer Johnson (Berkley PubGroup, 1983)

This book is an easy read, but a crucial one. It contains the parable of a young man in search of world-class management skills. It covers goal-setting, motivating, training, praising, and reprimanding employees. The book also explains the organizational science behind the reasons that such simple techniques work so effectively.

The 80/20 Principle: The Secret to Success by Achieving More with Less by Richard Koch (New York: Doubleday, 1999)

This is the book that first showed us how 80 percent of our success comes from 20 percent of our effort. Every business owner should read this to find out how to achieve more with less!

The Pursuit of Wow: Every Person's Guide to Topsy-Turvy Times by Tom Peters (New York: Vintage Books, 1994)

Do you stand out from your competitors? Do your customers say "Wow!" every time they interact with you? Tom Peters shows you why it's critical to excel at customer service to survive.

The Seven Habits of Highly Effective People by Stephen R. Covey (New York: Simon and Schuster, 1990)

Covey has studied the habits that are common among the world's most successful people and has distilled them down into integrated principles. A fantastic guide to living with fairness, integrity, honesty, and human dignity — principles that will set you and your business apart.

Who Moved My Cheese?: An Amazing Way to Deal with Change in Your Work and in Your Life by Spencer Johnson (New York: G.P. Putnam's Sons, 1998)

This quick read (only 96 pages) uses the metaphor of mice in a box who always know where their cheese is. But what happens when the cheese is moved? It is an outstanding look at change management and how to deal with the surprises life brings us all.

Other Titles Available at Your Local Bookstore and at www.self-counsel.com

Divorce Dollars

Akeela Davis

ISBN: 978-1-55180-851-2

$14.95 USD /$17.95 CAD

- Demonstrates how everyone can overcome the financial challenges of divorce
- Written by a financial planner

At least 40 percent of all new marriages today will end in divorce. The financial consequences of divorce can be traumatic. Many people who get divorced are left with little money, no income, and no credit rating. In some cases, if one partner looked after all the family's finances, the other partner is left unprepared and overwhelmed by the financial consequences of divorce.

Divorce Dollars is a complete guide to financial planning, demonstrating in a step-by-step manner how to overcome the financial challenges of divorce and lead a financially healthy life.

The book addresses everything from dividing the assets to retirement planning. By using examples of real people, Akeela Davis demonstrates how everyone can handle the financial challenges of divorce using careful planning and money smarts.

101 SMALL BUSINESS

PRICING STRATEGIES FOR SMALL BUSINESS

Andrew Gregson, BA, MA, MSc (ECON)

- Determine the right price for your product or service
- Improve the bottom line of your small business

Self-Counsel Press BUSINESS SERIES

Pricing a product or service can make or break a small business.

It's essential to use a good pricing strategy to ensure the products or services are appealing to customers and to ensure that the company is profitable. It's not always as simple as "the lowest price wins."

Pricing Strategies for Small Business covers the many different pricing strategies and helps readers to determine which methods are best for their small businesses. An optimal pricing strategy will depend on more than just the business costs. Forces within a business environment such as competitors, suppliers, availability of substitute products, and customers' disposable income all come into play.

Like all books from Self-Counsel Press, this book is written in an easy-to-understand manner. It shows readers step by step how to choose the right prices for their products and services, and covers the following topics:

- Psychological pricing
- Price skimming
- Penetration pricing
- Cost plus markup
- Multiple unit pricing